Law Essentials

INTERNATIONAL LAW

Law Essentials

INTERNATIONAL LAW

John P Grant
Professor of Law at Lewis & Clark Law School,
Portland, Oregon,
and
Professor Emeritus of International Law,
University of Glasgow

DUNDEE UNIVERSITY PRESS
2010

First edition published in Great Britain in 2010 by
Dundee University Press
University of Dundee
Dundee DD1 4HN

www.dup.dundee.ac.uk

ISBN 978 1 84586 114 8

No natural forests were destroyed to make this product; only farmed timber was used and
replanted.

British Library Cataloguing-in-Publication Data
A catalogue record for this book is available on request from the British Library

Typeset by Waverley Typesetters, Warham, Norfolk
Printed and bound by Bell & Bain Ltd, Glasgow

CONTENTS

TABLE OF CASES

TABLE OF INTERNATIONAL INSTRUMENTS

Specialist International Law Sources

CTS	Consolidated Treaty Series (1648–1918)
ETS	European Treaty Series
ILM	International Legal Materials
LNTS	League of Nations Treaty Series
UN Doc	United Nations Document
UNTS	United Nations Treaty Series

TABLE OF STATUTES

1 NATURE AND HISTORY OF INTERNATIONAL LAW

NATURE OF INTERNATIONAL LAW

Definition

International law is that body of legal principles and rules governing the activities of States and of other entities subject to it. A traditional definition of international law would have provided that it governed the relations of States to one another, with no reference to any other entities that might be subject to its principles and rules. The emergence of some rights and duties for international organisations, particularly the United Nations, and for individuals, particularly in the area of human rights, has led to an expansion of the definition to include these entities. But it always has been – and remains – primarily a system of law among States.

The term "international law" was first coined by Jeremy Bentham in 1789, and came to replace the earlier appellation of "law of nations". Both are, in a sense, misnomers, as international law is not concerned with nations, but rather with States. So, while the Scots – and the English, Welsh and Northern Irish – can rightly regard themselves as nations, none of them is a State; the State for these nations is the United Kingdom.

International law falls to be contrasted with municipal or domestic law, the law applicable in each State. In many States, for example federal States and even the United Kingdom, there is more than one system of municipal law. What is relevant to international law is that the UK, the State for international purposes, has a system (in fact, three systems) of municipal law that, at one and the same time, is a pre-condition to Statehood and is capable of implementing in the UK the obligations of international law.

Distinctive features of international law

There is no escaping the fact that international law is quite different from municipal law. Municipal legal systems typically have constitutions, but there is no world constitution. The closest to a world constitution is the Charter of the United Nations, but that is in reality no more than a super-treaty by which States have charged an international organisation and its organs with various tasks and over which States retain enormous control.

Municipal legal systems typically have legislatures charged with enacting laws. There is no international legislature. The closest to an international legislature is the UN General Assembly, but it has no power to enact laws binding on all States. Municipal legal systems typically have a system of courts with jurisdiction over disputes arising among the population and within the territory of each State. There is an International Court of Justice, but it does not have compulsory jurisdiction over States.

While municipal legal systems typically regulate huge numbers of people (China has a population of 1.3 billion, the UK 61 million), the community of States regulated by international law numbers only 192, being the number of members of the United Nations, plus, at most a few other entities with all the attributes of Statehood that are not UN members – the Republic of China (Taiwan), the Holy See and, possibly, Palestine and Kosovo.

The sources of law in municipal legal systems are typically the constitution, legislation and decided cases. The principal sources of international law, treaties and custom, are quite different in nature from municipal legal sources. They are consensual, that consent being express in treaties and implied in custom.

But is it law?

Far too much time, effort and paper have been devoted by international lawyers to countering the claim that international law is not law at all. If that claim were true, this book would end here ... for international law would have no place in the *Law Essentials* series.

International law *is* different from municipal law and, as most definitions of law are derived from the characteristics of municipal law, it is hardly surprising that international law falls short of some definitions of law. The influential John Austin defined law in 1832 as commands of a sovereign who is habitually obeyed accompanied by sanctions in the event of any breach. As international law does not consist of commands from a sovereign and of clear sanctions in the event of any breach, it does not, therefore, qualify as law. To Austin, international law was not law properly so called, but rather "law by close analogy" or "positive morality".

International law establishes norms which States regard as binding on them in their dealings with one another. What international law most clearly lacks is enforcement of its rules through the standard mechanism available in municipal law, namely courts. The World Court was created only in 1920 and is restricted to deciding cases where both disputant States have consented to jurisdiction.

Because of the limited role of the World Court and judicial settlement, international law has developed other methods by which its rules can be enforced. In excess of 90 per cent of international disputes are settled by direct negotiations between the States concerned. Some disputes are settled by mediation or conciliation. Some disputes are referred by the States concerned for settlement by arbitration.

Instead of asking early 19th-century legal philosophers whether international law is law, ask instead someone who practises international law in the 21st century. Ask those international legal practitioners whether they are applying law or positive morality. Look at the way international disputes are presented and argued to see whether international law is used in a manner similar to the way municipal law is used in municipal disputes. The conclusion from these analyses would be that international law is law, but not law in exactly the same way as municipal law is law.

The extension of international law

In its early days, international law extended to a few areas only. Rules were accepted by States about the inviolability of diplomatic envoys, authority over areas of sea and the effect of treaties – and not much more. From the early years of the 20th century, particularly since 1945, there has been an enormous extension of international law. That extension has been horizontal in the dual sense that more States have emerged on to the international arena and international law has developed to embrace areas previously regarded as within the exclusive purview of States. That extension has also been vertical in the sense that a substantial *corpus* of international law is now intended to affect individuals within States.

After the consolidation of States (mainly in Germany and Italy) in the 19th century, there were about 50 States in the world. The United Nations had 51 original Member States in 1945 and now has 192. While the total number of States remains small, the four-fold increase over the last 100 years has introduced into the international arena new States that do not necessarily subscribe to the values and standards of their long-established counterparts.

Alongside this increase in the number of international actors, the substantive scope of international law has been extended. Almost exclusively through multilateral treaties, international law has had its rules codified and improved from the previous broad and sometimes vague customs and, at the same time, new areas have been included within the ambit of international law. Areas previously thought to be within the exclusive province of States (for example human rights and economic affairs) are now subject to international regulation.

These new areas of international concern and regulation have resulted in a vertical penetration of international law into States, conferring rights and sometimes duties on individuals within States. This is in marked contrast to earlier international law which regulated the activities of States *inter se* and regarded the internal affairs of States as completely off-limits.

Law and politics

All law is heavily influenced by politics. By and large, municipal law emerges from a legislature in which politics are dominant. International law emerges from a process in which politics are predominant. In the context of international law, the term "politics" means something more than the party politics that dominates municipal affairs; it means the politics of the State which will, of course, be affected by party politics, but which becomes magnified and consolidated into the foreign policy of the State.

Those who create international law through their agreements and practices (States), being limited in number and well set in the belief in their sovereign independence, are loathe to surrender anything towards any compromise that is not in their clear interests. Negotiating multilateral treaties can, as a consequence, be a long and laborious business; the UN Convention on the Law of the Sea of 1982 took 9 years of intensive negotiation.

If getting States to concede anything towards a common accord is difficult, getting States to agree to concerted action can prove impossible. The 1999 NATO airstrikes against Serb targets to relieve the humanitarian catastrophe in Kosovo were undertaken without any legal justification. In 2003, a coalition led by the United States invaded Iraq, ostensibly to force Iraqi compliance with earlier Security Council resolutions. In both these situations, the politics of the major powers – their foreign policy imperatives – differed; and, as a consequence, the Security Council was unable to discharge the functions envisaged for it in the UN Charter.

What role, then, does international law play in States' foreign policy decisions? While many would like to think that legality should prevail over politics, in truth international law may be hugely influential but is not decisive in these decisions.

HISTORY OF INTERNATIONAL LAW

Early times

International lawyers like to glory in the antiquity of their discipline. They point, in particular, to the rules governing the relations of the ancient Greek city-States and the rules applicable in the Roman empire. Neither of these phenomena applied to entities outside the circle of the city-States and the Roman empire. Such rules as existed in those early days – such as on the inviolability of envoys and the sanctity of treaties – were founded on enlightened self-interest and reciprocity.

International law, in the form we know it today, emerged in the 17th century. If we are seeking a date for this beginning of "modern" international law, we can select either 1625 or 1648.

1625 and Grotius

Hugo de Groot (1583–1645), better known as Grotius, was a Dutch prodigy who, in 1625, published his *De Jure Belli ac Pacis* (*On the Laws of War and Peace*). Grotius has come to be regarded as the father of international law. His major contribution was that he systematised international law, breaking international law as it existed in his lifetime down into its component parts and applying appropriate rules to these parts. In his writings, he drew on natural law, as had many of his predecessors, but to that he added rules derived from treaties and the practice of States (custom).

1648 and Westphalia

At the end of the bloody Thirty Years War, the Peace of Westphalia was negotiated through two diplomatic congresses and resulted in the new political order based upon sovereign States. Thereafter, States, sovereign in themselves and led by a sovereign, became the building blocks of international society and international law.

Writings

Most legal systems in their early formative years rely heavily on the writings of scholars. International law is no less indebted to the work of scholars.

These scholars can be grouped into camps or schools. Early writers, such as the two Spanish theologians, Francico de Vitoria and Francisco Suarez, viewed the regulation of international affairs through the lens of natural law. Later adherents to natural law, such as Samuel von Pufendorf and Christian Wolff, came to view natural law as law rationally determined, derived from the nature of humankind as rational beings.

In the late 18th century, legal thinking shifted along with general political philosophy towards positivistic theories. The works of Emer de Vattel and Immanuel Kant focused on State practice to the exclusion of natural law. States mattered – and it is what States did that mattered. That concentration on States and their practice as the basis of international law prevailed into the 20th century, when there was a renaissance of natural law. Texts written today concede the primary place of States in the international system, but add roles for international organisations and individuals, and address issues unthinkable for a writer 100 years ago. The international protection of human rights for all and increasing concern for the environment are the supreme expressions of natural law in the period after 1945. Ironically, the protection of human rights and the environment has been effected through positivistic means, mainly treaties and, to a lesser extent, custom.

18th and 19th centuries

These 200 years saw a substantial expansion and consolidation of international legal rules. In particular, it was during this period that legal rules governing the sea became well established. Easier communications and increased interactions between States and nationals of States led to the development of diplomatic and consular law and to the law of State responsibility.

After the Napoleonic wars, the Congress of Vienna in 1815 was intended to secure the long-term peace of Europe and establish regular meetings of European States. The clear benefits of regular meetings between the powers resulted in two critical developments for international law: the use of multilateral Conventions and the creation of international organisations. The scope of multilateral Conventions, used previously for alliances and ending wars, became extended to such matters as the navigation on the Rhine and the Danube and the construction and status of the Suez Canal. Towards the end of the 19th century, multilateral Conventions began to regulate such matters as North Sea fisheries, the protection of submarine cables and slavery and the slave trade.

International co-operation on the use of rivers required some permanent organisations to undertake the necessary functions to ensure free and safe navigation, and the very first international organisations, the Rhine and the Danube Commissions, were created. There followed a number of other international organisations with essentially administrative functions – the International Telegraph Union in 1865 (still extant as the International Telecommunication Union) and the Universal Postal Union in 1874.

The 20th century therefore began with the realisation that multilateral Conventions could serve useful purposes as vehicles for international co-operation and for setting international standards; and that permanent international organisations, rather than *ad hoc* or irregular meetings between States, could perform valuable functions beyond the scope of any single State.

The League of Nations era

As a reaction to the carnage of World War I, the peace negotiators included in the peace settlement of 1919 a treaty establishing the first global international organisation with general competence: the League of Nations. The League was intended to prevent a repetition of the events that had happened in Europe between 1914 and 1918. As there was a repetition of these events a mere 20 years later, the League failed, and its failure can be attributed to the decentralised security system written into the Covenant and the recalcitrance of its members. It may have been a noble experiment that failed, but the lessons learned from that failure were incorporated in the Charter of its successor, the United Nations.

Nonetheless, if the League years (1920–45) did not consolidate a better world order, they were immensely important for international law. Attempts were made to outlaw war, obliquely through the League's Covenant and more directly through the Kellogg–Briand Pact of 1928. The earlier laws of war, found defective in World War I, were recast in 1929 in two new Conventions. The use of multilateral Conventions increased, the subject-matter ranging from international waterways (1921), maritime ports (1923) and international straits (1936) through the regulation of opium (1925), slavery (1926) and trafficking in women (1933) to the very first Convention on terrorism (1937).

The United Nations era

Even before the end of World War II, the Allies had plans for the creation of a new global international organisation to replace the League of Nations. Fifty States met in San Francisco for 2 months in 1945, at the end of which they signed the UN Charter, which came into force on 24 October of that year. Apart from Taiwan, and the problematic cases of the Holy See, Kosovo and Palestine, the UN has universality of membership, something that the very European-oriented League of Nations never achieved.

The UN's primary purpose, like that of its predecessor, is the maintenance of international peace and security. Learning from the experiences of the League, the UN Charter expressly prohibited the use or threat of military force (Art 2(4)) and set up a centralised mechanism through the Security Council to address threats to and breaches of the peace and acts of aggression (Chapter VII). The League's requirement of unanimity in voting in all its organs was replaced by a system of majority voting in the UN's organs. The competence of the UN's main deliberative organ, the General Assembly, was more widely expressed than that of the League's Assembly; it has, for instance, the power and the responsibility to "achieve international co-operation in solving international problems of an economic, social, cultural, or humanitarian character, and in promoting and encouraging respect for human rights and fundamental freedoms for all ..." (Art 1(3)).

Alongside the UN with its extensive competence, there are 16 autonomous mini-UNs, referred to as the Specialised Agencies, dealing with particular areas of international concern, ranging from labour and health standards (International Labour Organization and the World Health Organization) through international economic affairs (the World Bank Group of three organisations) to weather and tourism (World Meteorological Organization and World Tourism Organization).

There are now more than 300 intergovernmental organisations. Aside from global organisations, there has been a huge rise in the number of regional intergovernmental organisations. In Europe alone, there is the European Union, the European Economic Area, the Council of Europe, the North Atlantic Treaty Organizations and the Western European Union, to name only the leading organisations. Their work contributes to international law; the Council of Europe, for example, is the organisation responsible for the sophisticated European Convention on Human Rights of 1950.

The Permanent Court of International Justice, established in 1920, was replaced by the International Court of Justice but, name aside, the ICJ is essentially the same body, with the same Statute governing its activities and the same location at the Peace Palace in The Hague. The only difference is that, while the PCIJ was separate from the League, the ICJ is an integral part of the UN, its "principal judicial organ" (Art 92).

In the years since 1945, international law has expanded horizontally into areas such as human rights, international criminal law, international economic law and international environmental law. In 1947, the General Assembly established the International Law Commission, charged with the progressive development and codification of international law. Its law reform work has been hugely influential in the development of international law. In the last 60 years, the law has developed almost exclusively through multilateral treaties and through what has often been called "soft law": non-binding declarations, guidelines and standards that set norms that may become law by being adopted into treaties or crystallised into custom.

Essential Facts

- International law regulates the conduct of States in their dealings with one another.
- It is markedly different from municipal law, not least in lacking a court system to enforce its rules, as a result of which different procedures have been developed to resolve international disputes.
- International law as we know it today dates from the middle of the 17th century.
- The United Nations, set up in 1945, has been a major force in maintaining and restoring international peace and security *and* in developing international law.
- International law has, since 1945, extended its range to include such areas as human rights and its reach into States by establishing standards that have to be observed by States in their own law.

2 SOURCES OF INTERNATIONAL LAW

THE MEANING OF SOURCES

Sources as a term describes the font of, or the classification used for, the legal rules that are to be applied to a particular problem. The sources of international law are generally accepted as being expressed in Art 38(1) of the Statute of the International Court of Justice, which reads:

> "The Court, whose function is to decide in accordance with international law such disputes as are submitted to it, shall apply:
>
> a. international conventions, whether general or particular, establishing rules expressly recognized by the contesting states;
>
> b. international custom, as evidence of a general practice accepted as law;
>
> c. the general principles of law recognized by civilized nations;
>
> d. subject to the provisions of Article 59, judicial decisions and the teachings of the most highly qualified publicists of the various nations, as subsidiary means for the determination of rules of law.
>
> 2. This provision shall not prejudice the power of the Court to decide a case *ex aequo et bono*, if the parties agree thereto."

This article in the ICJ Statute is a direction to the International Court as to the law it is to apply. It is not stated to be an enumeration of the sources of international law. Yet no-one disputes that the listing in Art 38(1) is anything other than a listing of recognised sources of international law. The only question is whether Art 38(1) exhaustively lists the sources of international law or whether there are other sources not mentioned in that article.

A distinction is sometimes drawn between the formal and the material sources of international law. Article 38(1)(a)–(c) (Conventions, custom and general principles) are the formal sources; they are where one turns for the actual content of the law. Article 38(1)(d) (judicial decisions and teachings), expressly described as "subsidiary means for the determination of the rules of law", are material sources in the sense that they are not the law, but merely evidence of the law, that law being Conventions, custom or general principles – the three formal sources.

Does Art 38(1) represent a hierarchy, with Conventions taking precedence over custom and general principles and custom over general principles? In theory, all the formal sources of international law are equal, so, in theory, no one formal source can take precedence over another. The Geneva Conventions on the Territorial Sea and on the High Seas of 1958 between them made it abundantly clear that no State could claim an exclusive fishing zone outside the limits of its territorial sea; the international community had no difficulty, a mere 20 years later, conceding that States could claim exclusive fishing zones of 200 miles from the coast as customary law. The formal sources being equal, the later in time prevails – referred to as the principle *lex posterior derogat priori*. However, common sense dictates that, when faced with an international law issue, one should first look to any applicable Convention, then to any relevant custom and, failing both these, to general principles of law.

The power of the Court to determine a case *ex aequo et bono* if the parties agree under Art 38(2) allows the Court to ignore the legal rules set out in Art 38(1), using instead equity and fairness and justice; it has never been requested by the parties to any case before the Court, and so is untested.

CONVENTIONS

The Vienna Convention

While Art 38(1)(a) uses the term "conventions", the more usual term is "treaties". The law of treaties evolved through customary law and, thanks to the work of the International Law Commission, was codified into a treaty (a treaty on treaties), the Vienna Convention on the Law of Treaties of 1969 ("VCLT"). Article 2(1)(a) of the VCLT defines a treaty as "an international agreement concluded between States in written form and governed by international law".

That definition means that, for a treaty where one of the parties is not a State (an international organisation, for example), the provisions of the VCLT do not apply. Indeed, a later Vienna Convention in 1986, the Vienna Convention on the Law of Treaties between States and International Organizations and between International Organizations, though not yet in force, has provisions similar to the 1969 Vienna Convention for treaties where at least one of the parties is an international organisation.

That definition also means that an unwritten treaty is not regulated by the provisions of the VCLT. An unwritten treaty will, if seriously intentioned and capable of clear proof, create legal obligation. Some writers have thought that, when Nils Claus Ihlen, the Norwegian Foreign

Minister, stated publicly in 1919 that Norway would "make no difficulty" to Denmark's claim to Greenland, he was entering some kind of oral treaty with Denmark. In the *Eastern Greenland Case* (1933), the World Court ruled that the Ihlen declaration constituted not a treaty, but a unilateral legally binding obligation on Norway not to contest Denmark's claim to Greenland. Likewise, when Australia and New Zealand sought a declaration from the Court that France's atmospheric nuclear testing in the South Pacific was contrary to international law, the Court decided that there was no need for any such declaration as France had publicly stated its intention to cease atmospheric nuclear testing: *Nuclear Test Cases* (1974). The Ihlen and French declarations created binding legal obligations, but they were not oral treaties.

A distinction is sometimes drawn between a law-making treaty (*traité-loi*) and a treaty-contract (*traité-contrat*), the former being large multilateral agreements on matters of importance, the latter being agreements with a small number of parties on specific matters. Some think that a *traité-loi* is a general source of law in the same manner as legislation in municipal law, while a *traité-contrat* is, like a municipal contract, merely an agreement between limited parties for limited purposes and not general law. However attractive this distinction may appear, it is not sound. All treaties are contracts between parties and all treaties create law, but only for the consenting parties. Article 34 of the VCLT confirms the long-standing rule that a treaty creates neither rights nor duties for a third State without its consent.

The elements of treaty law

Treaties are to international law what contracts are to municipal law, and the rules governing treaties are similar to those governing municipal contracts. The VCLT makes provision for the conclusion of treaties (Arts 6–18), for their invalidity on the grounds of error, fraud, corruption or coercion (Arts 46–53) and for their termination on the grounds of material breach or impossibility of performance (Arts 54–72). In all these provisions, the international rules would be familiar to any municipal lawyer.

There are, however, some aspects of international treaty law that differ from municipal contract law. Many treaties require a two-stage process of approval. In such cases, signature of the text of a treaty signifies merely that the negotiators accept the text as authentic (Art 10); the treaty is binding on a State only after subsequent ratification (Art 14). This two-stage process allows each State a pause for deliberation on whether it wishes to be bound by the terms of the treaty. While no State is obliged to ratify a treaty, and a treaty becomes binding only on ratification, a signatory State must do nothing to defeat the object and purpose of the treaty (Art 18). Ratification is regulated by a State's constitution. In the UK, the Westminster Government ratifies treaties on its own without any reference to Parliament; in the US, the Constitution requires that the advice and consent of the Senate be obtained before the executive can ratify treaties.

For most municipal contracts, there is no requirement that they should be registered anywhere. Such was the concern in the international community about secret treaties, especially secret alliances, that there have been requirements in international law about the registration (and publication) of treaties since the days of the League of Nations. Article 102 of the UN Charter demands that all treaties entered into by Member States be registered with the Secretariat; the sanction for failure to register is that an unregistered treaty cannot be invoked before any organ of the UN, including, of course, the International Court of Justice. Registered treaties are published in hard copy in the *United Nations Treaty Series* (UNTS), now running to over 2,400 volumes, and online at http://treaties.un.org.

One of the most vexed issues in treaty law concerns reservations. A State may wish to become a party to a treaty, but also wish to be excluded from the application of some part(s) of the treaty; that State will then enter a reservation, stating that it does not consider itself bound by the part(s) it dislikes. The basic treaty rule, like the equivalent municipal contract rule, is clear: a treaty once agreed has to be accepted in its entirety, without reservation, and any proposed reservation has to be agreed by all the other contracting parties. This basic rule is easy to apply to bilateral treaties, where any reservation is really a counter-offer to be accepted (or not) by the other party.

In the *Reservations to the Genocide Convention Case* (1951), the International Court decided that the basic rule was not appropriate for a multilateral treaty like the Genocide Convention of 1948. The Genocide Convention, with its important humanitarian purpose and universal application, the Court said, should not be stymied by a rule that might have excluded some States for entering a minor reservation. The Court crafted a new rule. When a State enters a reservation, it is for the other parties to the treaty, individually, to determine whether the reservation is minor ("compatible with the object and purpose of the treaty") and to decide whether the reserving State is to be a party. This new rule was stated by the Court to apply only to the special circumstances of the Genocide Convention, but it rapidly became accepted for all multilateral treaties. It was, with minor amendments, incorporated into the VCLT (Arts 19–23). The position now is that a State that makes a reservation to a multilateral treaty will be a party to the treaty without the reserved matter except in respect of any other party which objects to the reservation as incompatible with the object and purpose of the treaty *and* to the reserving State being a party.

One of the grounds for terminating or suspending a treaty has no counterpart in municipal contract law: fundamental change of circumstances. Article 62 of the VCLT restates an old rule, often referred to by the maxim *rebus sic stantibus*, that a treaty may end when there has been a fundamental and unanticipated change in the circumstances that were central to its initial conclusion. The ICJ has acknowledged that fundamental change of circumstances is an exceptional basis for terminating treaties: *Fisheries Jurisdiction Cases (Jurisdiction)* (1974); *Gabčikovo Nagymaros Project Case* (1997). In the former case, the Court did not accept that increased fishing technology and the consequent depletion of fish stocks was fundamental so as to terminate a 1961 treaty on fishery limits; and in the latter, the Court did not think that political, economic and environmental circumstances had changed so fundamentally as to terminate a 1977 treaty for a joint hydro-electric dam project.

Two fundamental principles of treaty law are worthy of special note. The first is the principle embodied in Art 26 of the VCLT, known as *pacta sunt servanda*: "Every treaty in force is binding upon the parties to it, and must be performed by them in good faith." The second is the set of rules for interpreting treaties. According to Art 31(1) of the VCLT, the general rule is that "a treaty shall be interpreted in good faith in accordance with the ordinary meaning to be given to the terms of the treaty in their context and in the light of its object and purpose". According to Art 32, where that general rule would leave the meaning ambiguous or obscure or lead to a manifestly absurd or unreasonable result, recourse can be had to supplementary means of interpretation, including the preparatory work of the treaty, called the *travaux préparatoires*, or, in American parlance, the legislative history of the treaty.

CUSTOM

Custom is the oldest, and at one time the dominant, source of international law. Much of the content of contemporary international law started as custom; some has been codified into treaties, while some remains custom. The rules on diplomatic and consular relations began and evolved as custom before being codified in treaties in 1961 and 1963. The law of the sea likewise began and evolved as custom, before being codified in treaties, first in 1958, then later in 1982. The law relating to State responsibility for international wrongs began, evolved and remains as custom. When international law has extended into new areas, such as human rights, economic affairs and the environment, it has invariably done so through multilateral treaties.

Article 38(1) of the ICJ Statute identifies its second formal source as "international custom, as evidence of a general practice accepted as law". In fact, it is a general practice accepted as law that constitutes the custom. Custom, then, is something that States do (or refrain from doing) generally, consistently and for some time that, somewhere along this general and consistent course of action, they come to regard as legally obligatory. That process can be represented as in Figure 1:

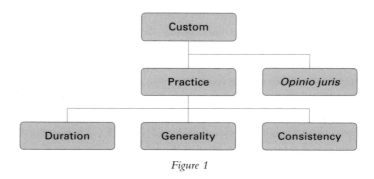

Figure 1

The principal component of custom is the practice of States. What they do, and refrain from doing, is critical to the formation of custom. How long they do it, how widely among the community of States they do it and how consistently they do it are the three elements that have to be established to elevate a practice to the level of custom.

Duration

At one time, it was thought that, for custom, a practice had to be followed from something like time immemorial. In the 19th century, it was suggested that in the order of 100 years was needed. Now, it is recognised that the duration element in custom is inextricably linked to the other two elements; custom can emerge quickly if the majority of States consistently follow a practice.

The landmark *North Sea Continental Shelf Cases* (1969) demonstrate how quickly a custom can emerge. Prior to States claiming the oil and gas resources lying in the continental shelf off their coasts from the 1940s, it was clear that international law regarded these resources as located under the high seas (as indeed they were) and subject to either the high seas rule that they were not capable of national appropriation or were, like fish, open to capture by any State. By the early 1950s, two arbitrations demonstrated that there was no established custom whereby a coastal State had exclusive right to the natural resources of its continental shelf. This right was recognised in the Geneva Convention on the Continental Shelf of 1958. In 1969, when considering a case involving the boundary between the continental shelf of West Germany, the Netherlands and Denmark, the ICJ had no difficulty in saying that the exclusive right of a State in its continental shelf was part of customary law. Even allowing for the fact that the custom had been speeded by the adoption of the Geneva Convention, it nonetheless emerged in less than 30 years.

Some theorists talk of "instant custom", meaning rules of customary law created by immediate consensus among States around a particular practice. So, it is argued, when the General Assembly adopts a resolution, intended to set norms and expressed in clear language, that resolution, if supported by an overwhelming majority of the Assembly's members, can be regarded as custom. Instant custom is intended to counter the relative slowness of the creation of regular custom in a rapidly changing world. There is no doubt that General Assembly resolutions may express existing customary rules or may contribute to the emergence of a custom, but they cannot be instant custom.

Generality

To be custom, a practice must also be generally followed by States. International law does not require that all States follow a practice – merely that there be a substantial number of States acting in conformity. Article 38(1)(b) talks of "general" practice, not universal practice. In theory, it does not matter whether the States following a practice are major or minor international powers, all States being regarded as equal. In practice, the tendency is to look to the practice of the major players in the relevant area. So, in inquiring whether a rule relating to the sea was custom, particular regard would be had to the practice of the leading maritime powers.

If a practice is followed in a region or locality, but not universally, there is the possibility of the emergence of a local custom. While universal custom, once established, is intended to bind all States, local custom is more contractual and binds only those States that follow it. So, when Colombia claimed that there was a local custom allowing it to characterise a Peruvian dissident as a political offender and therefore entitled to safe passage out of Peru, the ICJ held that there was no such custom at all because there was no generality of practice even among Latin American States and, significantly for an alleged local custom, the practice had not been followed by Peru: *Asylum Case* (1950).

Consistency

Just as custom requires that the generality of States follow a practice, so it requires consistency in what they do. In the *Asylum Case*, the Court, looking for a "constant and uniform usage", could find only "so much uncertainty and contradiction, so much fluctuation and discrepancy" that there was no custom on diplomatic asylum as claimed by Colombia. The issue of consistency was directly addressed in the *Military and Paramilitary Activities Case* (1986), where the Court said that "complete consistency" and "absolute rigorous conformity" were not required; what was required was that State practice "should, in general, be consistent ... , in that instances of State conduct inconsistent with a given rule should generally have been treated as breaches of the rule, not as indications of the recognition of a new rule".

Opinio juris

Opinio juris is the Latin tag (in full, *opinio juris sive necessitatis*) for what Art 38(1)(b) of the ICJ Statute refers to as "accepted as law". It is the psychological element in custom. It is the belief in States that, in following a particular practice, they are doing so out of a sense of obligation. And, most importantly, it is the element that converts a practice that is long enough, general enough and consistent enough into custom.

In the *North Sea Continental Shelf Cases*, there was, the ICJ thought, sufficient *opinio juris* from the claims made by States to the continental shelf and from the Geneva Convention on the Continental Shelf to establish some general customary rules, but insufficient *opinio juris* to allow the Convention's rule on continental shelf boundaries to be part of customary law – not least because the motives of those States which had made the boundary agreements cited to the Court were unclear, some already being bound by the Geneva Convention's rule and others possibly intending to acceded to the Convention. In considering whether custom prohibited a State from prosecuting a foreigner for a crime committed in a collision on the high seas, the PCIJ in the *Lotus Case* (1927) determined that there was no such custom, partly because it was by no means clear that there were very few prosecutions because States thought that they were prohibited by custom from doing so.

As with all law, the burden of proving a rule of law falls on the party relying on it, so the burden of proving custom falls upon the State seeking to found on it. It may be reasonably simple to prove the practice element in custom, but it is difficult to identify the motive that States might have in following a particular practice. States do not always explain why they follow a course of action; and, even when they do, that information is not readily available throughout the international community. In the *Military and Paramilitary Activities Case*, the Court said that *opinio juris* "may be deduced from, *inter alia*, the attitude of the Parties towards certain General Assembly resolutions. ... The effect of consent to the text of such resolutions ... may be understood as an acceptance of the validity of the rule or set of rules declared by the resolution by themselves". If States generally and consistently follow a practice for a substantial length of time, it is not unreasonable to presume that they are following that practice out of a sense of obligation. The problems of establishing *opinio juris*, while difficult, are not insurmountable.

Custom and treaties

There is a synergy between custom and treaties. Much of what was once custom is now enshrined in treaties. But there is movement the other way too. The adoption of the Geneva Convention on the Continental Shelf in 1958 undoubtedly speeded up the process whereby the customary rules on the continental shelf emerged; and the Convention's terms had a precision that could readily be used as the customary rules. While the international rules on genocide, war crimes and crimes against humanity all first appeared in treaties, few would now deny that they are now part of customary law too.

Yet, the content of a treaty rule and a customary rule on the same issue might not be identical. In the *Military and Paramilitary Activities Case*, the Court, recognising that a treaty rule (Art 51 of the UN Charter) and customary rule on the right of self-defence co-existed, and that the later treaty rule did not subsume or override the customary rule, said: "The areas covered by the two sources do not overlap exactly, and the rules do not have the same content." There can readily be rules emanating from treaties and custom, identical or different in content, governing the same situation, the treaty rule applying to those States bound by the treaty, the customary rule applying to those States which are not so bound.

The best (and worst) example of the synergy is in the field of human rights, where the content of the myriad of treaties is often stated as being custom, extending that content beyond the treaties' contracting parties to the entire community of States. It might be a useful tool for human rights activists to claim that all that is in human rights treaties is also custom, but it is manifestly wrong in law. Can it seriously be contended that, as there are treaty prohibitions on the death penalty in Europe and in the Second Optional Protocol to the International Covenant on Civil and Political Rights, the 50 per cent of States that are not parties to these instruments and that retain the death penalty are in breach of customary international law?

GENERAL PRINCIPLES OF LAW

The third formal source of international law, and clearly subordinate to treaties and custom, is "the general principles of law recognized by civilized nations". There has been some controversy as to what this term means. To some, it means the general principles of international law. However, a better understanding of what is intended in Art 38(1)(c) of the ICJ Statute can be gained by examining the genesis of that article. Article 38 was first drafted in 1920 as the sources article in the Statute of the Permanent Court of International Justice and survived, unchanged and in its entirety, as the sources article of the Statute of the International Court of Justice. Article 38(1)(c) dates therefore from the early 20th century, an era in which there was a belief that, in the absence of an applicable treaty or relevant custom, an international tribunal should decline to give a decision. This belief is often expressed as the doctrine of *non liquet* (it is not clear). While the doctrine is patent nonsense, for a tribunal usually requires the applicant State to prove the facts and law of its claim, failure to do both resulting in the dismissal of the claim, the idea of *lacunae* (or gaps) in international law gained traction.

Realising that treaties and custom might not provide answers to all disputes submitted to the Permanent Court, the drafters of the Statute added a third source designed to fill gaps in the law. That was, and still is, Art 38(1)(c). The intention was, and still is, that gaps were to be filled by resort to principles of law common in municipal legal systems. The reference to "civilized nations" was meant to refer to mature and developed legal system, and not primitive and undeveloped systems; and the term, offensive and inappropriate in a post-colonial era, can safely be ignored.

General principles of law are therefore those rules which prevail in most, but not necessarily all, municipal legal systems. As the International Court said in the *Barcelona Traction Company Case* (1970), in identifying what measure of diplomatic protection is afforded under international law to limited companies, a matter not regulated by treaties or custom, "It is to the rules generally accepted by municipal legal systems ... , and not to the municipal law of a particular State" of which the Court had to take cognisance.

The Court has utilised general principles to determine the international rule that reparation is due for any internationally wrongful act (*Chorzow*

Factory (Indemnity) Case (Merits) (1928); that a State may be personally barred (estopped) from insisting on a claim by its own actions (*Temple of Preah Vihear Case* (1962)); that circumstantial evidence is admissible in deciding on a State's alleged wrongdoing (*Corfu Channel Case* (1949)); and that a case once decided between the same parties on the same facts cannot be raised again, commonly called the *res judicata* principle (*Effect of Awards of the UN Administrative Tribunal Case* (1954)).

SUBSIDIARY SOURCES

Judicial decisions

"Judicial decisions" are stated in Art 38(1)(d) of the ICJ Statute to be one of the (two) subsidiary means for determining the rules of international law. Thus expressed, judicial decisions are at most a material source of international law, not a source in their own right, but merely applications of the formal sources. The qualification that judicial decisions are subsidiary sources subject to Art 59 of the Statute (which imports the *res judicata* principle into the ICJ) means that the decisions in the mind of the drafters of the provision are those of the World Court itself. It is its decisions that provide evidence of the treaties, custom and general principles that make up the *corpus* of international law.

In practice, decisions of the ICJ, though small in number, are of substantial importance to the development of international law. While the Court does not operate any kind of common-law system of binding precedent, and does not draw any clear distinction between the *ratio decidendi* of its decisions and the *obiter dicta* of its judges, its decisions exercise considerable influence as an impartial and well-considered statement of the law by jurists of authority made in the light of actual problems which arise before them. The Court also practices what is called judicial consistency, following its earlier decisions without regarding itself as slavishly bound to do so – demonstrated clearly in its enunciation of the customary rule on delimiting continental shelf boundaries (equitable principles using all relevant circumstances) in the *North Sea Continental Shelf Cases* in 1969 and its application of that same rule in eight subsequent disputes with quite different fact patterns.

The judicial decisions of international arbitrations and municipal courts are clearly not intended as subsidiary sources of international law. International arbitrations frequently decide disputes on the basis of international law and their awards are treated as authoritative evidence of international law. A 1928 arbitration, the *Island of Palmas Arbitration*, clearly enunciated the (customary) rules on the acquisition by a State of territory. Decisions of municipal courts may be used as evidence of State practice and of a State's attitude to practice; and they may also, in applying international law rules in municipal disputes, elaborate and clarify these rules.

Writings

Legal scholarship, described in Art 38(1)(d) as "the teaching of the most highly qualified publicists of the various nations", is a subsidiary, and therefore material, source. International law relied heavily on writings in its early days, but the significance of legal scholarship is considerably less in today's more developed and sophisticated system. Particularly in relation to custom, where evidence of State practice is difficult to obtain, writings can show what a rule might be. In *The Paquete Habana* (1900), the US Supreme Court said that writings "are resorted to by judicial tribunals, not for the speculations of their authors concerning what the law ought to be, but for trustworthy evidence of what the law really is"; and in *The Franconia Case* (1876), an English court warned that "writers on international law, however valuable their labours may be in elucidating and ascertaining the principles and rules of law, cannot make the law. ... In the absence of proof of assent [by States], ... no unanimity on the part of theoretical writers would warrant the judicial application of the law on sole authority of their views or statements".

OTHER POSSIBLE SOURCES

Equity

While Art 38(1) does not expressly mention equity as one of the sources available to the Court, there is no question but that the it can use, and has used, equity, in the sense of fairness and justice. In the *North Sea Continental Shelf Cases*, the ICJ had no hesitation in stating that continental shelf boundary delimitations were to be made using equitable principles. Equity has also been employed in international arbitrations, and is sometimes stated to be a source that an arbitral tribunal is to apply. In the *Cayagu Indians Arbitration* (1926), the tribunal was so anxious to give justice to the Canadian Cayugas that it ignored the fact that there was no treaty between the US and UK giving them the right under international law to an annuity from the state of New York, saying that the award was "founded in the elementary principle of justice that requires us to look at the substance and not stick in the bark of the legal form".

There has been speculation about whether equity is an inherent part of international law and therefore needs no mention among the sources for it to be applied or whether equity is already included among the sources as a general principle of law. Support for the former view comes from the *North Sea Continental Shelf Case* when the Court said: "Whatever the legal reasoning of a court of justice, its decisions must be just, and therefore in that sense equitable." Support for the latter view comes from the application of the equitable rule that one party to a dispute cannot invoke the non-performance of a treaty by the other party as justification of its own non-performance in the *Diversion of the Waters of the River Meuse Case* (1937). Both views are tenable, as Judge Manley O Hudson pointed out in his separate opinion in the *River Meuse Case*: "It must be concluded, therefore, that under Article 38 of the Statute, if not independently of that Article, the Court has some freedom to consider principles of equity as part of the international law which it must apply."

General Assembly resolutions

The General Assembly has no legislative power; its resolutions are mere recommendations. However, it has, on occasion, adopted resolutions with a clear intention that they establish legal norms and with language that looks legislative. For example, in December 1948 the General Assembly adopted a resolution titled the "Declaration of Human Rights" ("UDHR"), stated in its preamble to be "a common standard of achievement" and containing 30 articles written in clear legislative language. The question arises as to the normative effect of resolutions of this type.

One school of thought argues that, as Art 38(1) of the ICJ Statute was drafted at a time when all resolutions of the Assembly of the League of Nations were adopted by unanimous vote (and therefore equivalent to treaties), and Art 38(1) was not amended to take account of majority voting in the UN General Assembly, there is a simple omission in the Statute and resolutions of the General Assembly, if in suitable language, should be regarded as a source of international law alongside treaties, custom and general principles.

The other school denies that resolutions can be sources in their own right, but this school does not deny the normative intention and effect of some resolutions. This school notes that some resolutions have had substantial normative effect and invariably cite the UDHR as an example; and then seeks to explain possible bases of that effect. The Friendly Relations Declaration of 1970 "solemnly proclaims" seven principles, all of them drawn from Art 2 of the UN Charter, fleshed out with more detail. In so far as these General Assembly principles are law, it is argued, they are law as an authoritative interpretation of the UN Charter. That argument becomes less sustainable for the UDHR because the Charter's reference to human rights is skeletal; all the Charter talks about is promoting human rights without mentioning what human rights might be. The 30 articles of the UDHR, therefore, can hardly be an authoritative interpretation of virtually nothing.

The better view is that General Assembly resolutions can reflect existing custom or express emerging custom. The UDHR was the basis of human right provisions put into many States constitutions after 1948 and was negotiated into two international covenants by 1966; therefore, its provisions contributed to the emergence of customary human rights and, indeed, its terms exactly express these rights. Likewise, the right to self-determination expressed in the 1960 Declaration on the Granting of Independence to Colonial Countries and Peoples, building on the barest mention in the Charter, became part of the decolonisation culture of the time and found its way into other international instruments; it also helped develop the custom. The 1962 Resolution on Permanent Sovereignty over Natural Resources set out rules on the expropriation that had long been thought to be the governing law; and the resolution's rules were endorsed as expressing custom in the *Texaco–Libya Arbitration* (1977).

Jus cogens and fundamental principles

The idea behind *jus cogens* was simple, but it has developed into something well beyond the intention of its proponents. Just as contracts in municipal law may be void because they contravene public policy or are immoral, so, it was suggested from the 1930s, that treaties should be void if they conflicted with some fundamental international norms. That sensible idea found its way into the Vienna Convention on the Law of Treaties, which provided that a treaty is void if, at the time of its conclusion, it conflicts with a peremptory norm of general international law (Art 53); and that the emergence of a new peremptory norm voids earlier inconsistent treaties (Art 64). For these purposes, a peremptory norm is "a norm accepted and recognized by the international community of States as a whole as a norm from which no derogation is permitted ...".

But what are peremptory norms? Most agree that the illegal use of force, the prohibitions on torture, genocide, slavery and egregious war crimes and inhibitions on the exercise of self-determination would be *jus cogens* norms. So, a treaty of alliance to attack and occupy a neighbouring country in order to install a new State religion would violate a *jus cogens* norm and be void, as would a bilateral treaty to permit interrogation techniques amounting to torture by one party of terrorist suspects who are nationals of the other party. But beyond these limited examples, what else constitutes a peremptory norm? The Friendly Relations Declaration of 1970 promulgated a number of rules of international law that States would consider as of fundamental importance: for instance, non-intervention in a State's internal affairs and non-interference with a State's territorial integrity and political independence. These must also be *jus cogens* norms, for no State would deny that these are duties accepted by the community of States as a whole from which no derogation is permitted. And, if these rules are *jus cogens*, what other rules?

Somehow, the *jus cogens* concept has migrated from the law of treaties to general international law. To many commentators, *jus cogens* is custom; but, more than regular custom, it is super-custom. On that analysis, there are rules of customary law that prevail over other customary rules. The ICJ got very close to acknowledging this in the *Western Sahara Case* (1975) when it allowed the right to self-determination of the Western Saharan people to prevail over customary rules invoked by Morocco and Mauritania to claim title to the territory of the Western Sahara.

THE INTERNATIONAL LAW COMMISSION

Established by a General Assembly resolution of 1947, to which is attached its Statute, the ILC consists of 34 experts in international law whose task is to undertake the progressive development of international law and its codification. The initial idea was that the ILC would progressively develop the rules of customary law where they were not sufficiently uniform or ripe for codification, but, where they were uniform and ripe, would prepare codifying Conventions for adoption at international conferences. However, this apparently clear theoretical distinction between progressive development and codification drawn in Art 15 of the ILC Statute becomes somewhat blurred in practice.

Nonetheless, in looking at the work of the Commission, there are two distinct lines in what is has achieved. The most obvious line, and for which it is most famous, is the elaboration of codifying treaties. The ILC drafted what became the four Geneva Conventions on the Law of the Sea of 1958, the Vienna Conventions on Diplomatic Relations of 1961 and on Consular Relations of 1963, the Vienna Convention on the Law of Treaties of 1969, the Statute of the International Criminal Court of 1998 and many others.

The other line is what might be called progressive development – investigation, study and reporting on areas of international law. There may be no ultimate outcome beyond a report or a set of draft articles, but this work has proved immensely valuable in collecting evidence of State practice and attempting to make sense of it. The law on State responsibility, one the most "customary" areas of international law, has been rendered into draft articles after extensive study ending in 2001; and, while unlikely ever to become a Convention, these draft articles declare the present state of the law and will shape its future development.

Some have said that the ILC is more important than the ICJ to international law. The ICJ decides such cases as are referred to it and, in doing so, declares what the existing law is. The ILC is the initiator of codifying Conventions and the declarer of the existing law – and its work extends over a wide range of issues that it wishes to investigate or the General Assembly instructs it to investigate.

SOFT LAW

In some areas of international law (international environmental law and some aspects of human rights), unratified treaties, declarations and other non-binding instruments have created commitments and aspirations that, while not themselves law (hard law), are regarded as soft law. This soft law, while not legally binding, sets norms and standards that may become crystallised into custom or adopted into treaties.

Essential Facts

- The principal sources of international law are treaties and custom; both are consensual, that consent being express in treaties and implied in custom.
- Treaty law is similar to municipal contract law.
- Custom is made up of what States actually do in their practice with one another in the belief that they are obliged to do so.
- General principles of law are rules of international law derived from rules commonly applicable in the municipal legal systems of the world.
- Some General Assembly resolutions, because of their intent and language, have normative effect in international law as expressions of existing or emerging custom.
- There are some (but only a few) fundamental rules of international law, called *jus cogens*, that override treaties and custom.

Essential Cases

Reservations to the Genocide Convention Case (1951): the ICJ held that the effect of a reservation to a multilateral Convention was to be determined by the other parties, who could regard the reservation as incompatible with the object and purpose of the Convention and the reserving State as not a party to the Convention.

North Sea Continental Shelf Cases (1969): the ICJ held that the general rules in the Geneva Convention on the Continental Shelf (1958) represented custom, but not the specific rules for delimiting a continental shelf boundary, where the applicable custom required an equitable solution having regard to all relevant circumstances.

Military and Paramilitary Activities Case (1986): in deciding that the US measures in support of the Contras in Nicaragua were unlawful, the ICJ held that, for custom, there must be substantial uniformity in what States did in practice, but not necessarily unanimity.

3 INTERNATIONAL LAW AND MUNICIPAL LAW

The relationship between international law and municipal law raises both theoretical and practical questions. Theoretically, the question is whether they are part of the same legal system or distinct legal systems. Practically, the question is the extent to which international law is part of municipal law.

MONISM AND DUALISM

Monism posits that international law and municipal law are part of the same legal system. As a consequence, rules of international law are automatically part of municipal law. One of the leading monists, Hans Kelsen, even went as far as arguing that law cascaded through international law to municipal from a common fundamental principle (a *Grundnorm*).

Dualism posits the more realistic position that international law and municipal law are distinct legal systems, largely because of the fundamental differences between them (as discussed in Chapter 1). As a consequence, rules of international law can become part of municipal law only if they are adopted or accepted into municipal law.

INTERNATIONAL LAW PERSPECTIVE

Given the essentially different subject–matter between international law and municipal law, there are very few occasions in which a municipal legal rule will be relevant for use in international law. Nonetheless, the possibility exists, through Art 38(1)(c) of the ICJ Statute, for general principles of municipal law to be sources of international law (see Chapter 2); and here the rule being imported into international law is a rule common to a vast number of States and not the municipal law of any one State.

There is a long-standing principle that, at the international level, international law prevails in all situations over municipal law. Article 13 of the Draft Declaration on the Rights and Duties of States of 1949 puts it succinctly:

> "Each State has the duty to carry out in good faith the obligations arising from treaties and other sources of international law, and it may not invoke provisions in its constitution or its laws as an excuse for failure to perform this duty."

Earlier, in the famous *Alabama Claims Arbitration* (1872), an international tribunal decided that Britain could not invoke the absence of legislation prohibiting the building and fitting-out of vessels in Liverpool for use by the Confederate forces during the American Civil War as a defence to the violation of its duty under international law as a neutral to assist neither side in the conflict. The Vienna Convention on the Law of Treaties of 1969 (in Art 27) applies the same principle to the law of treaties.

MUNICIPAL LAW PERSPECTIVE

Whether international law is part municipal law, and what effect it has in municipal law, is a matter for each State's constitutional arrangements. These arrangements may be monistic, allowing for the automatic incorporation of international rules, or dualistic, allowing international rules into municipal law only after some specific act of adoption. And, in this regard, most States draw a distinction between treaties and custom.

The United Kingdom

Treaties

As treaty-making falls within the prerogative power, and as such is undertaken exclusively by the Government, there is a strong constitutional objection to any treaty being automatically part of UK law. In constitutional theory, the legislative power is exclusively vested in Parliament. To allow any treaty to apply automatically in the UK would be equivalent to allowing the executive to legislate. In *Maclaine Watson & Co* v *Department of Trade and Industry* (1989), Lord Oliver said:

> "as a matter of the constitutional law of the United Kingdom, the royal prerogative, while it embraces the making of treaties, does not extend to altering the law or conferring rights on individuals or depriving individuals of rights which they enjoy in domestic law without the intervention of Parliament. ... Quite simply, a treaty is not part of English law unless and until it has been incorporated into the law by legislation".

So, in the famous *Parlement Belge* case (1879), the absence of legislation prevented a bilateral Convention between Belgium and the UK concluded for the specific purpose of granting immunity to State-owned vessels from applying to a Belgian-owned mail packet following a collision in the English Channel.

Of course, only treaties that intend some alteration in municipal law require enabling legislation if they are to have effect in UK law. Some treaties (for example of alliance or of peace) intend no change in UK law and, for them, enabling legislation is irrelevant. Enabling legislation is not the same as ratification, an act of definitive acceptance of a treaty within the exclusive purview of the Government.

In the UK constitutional system, the Government runs the risk of ratifying a treaty requiring some change in domestic law yet being unable to push the necessary enabling legislation through Parliament, leaving the UK in breach of the treaty. To minimise this risk, there was introduced in 1924 the Ponsonby constitutional convention whereby every treaty is laid before both Houses of Parliament for 21 days prior to ratification. This process was refined in 1997 with the attachment of an explanatory memorandum to each treaty laid under the Ponsonby convention, explaining the salient features of the treaty.

A particular problem arose on the UK's accession to the European Communities in the early 1970s. Under EC law, parts of the founding treaties, and some measures taken under the treaties, had to have direct application in all the Member States. There clearly was no reasonable prospect of applying the classic UK doctrine that treaties have no effect in the UK without enabling legislation. In a masterpiece of parliamentary draftsmanship, s 2 of the European Communities Act 1972 enabled existing directly applicable EC law and pre-enabled future directly applicable EC law.

Custom

While the UK adopts a dualistic approach to treaties, it has always been monistic when it comes to custom. There are reported cases from as early as the 18th century to the effect that custom is automatically part of municipal law. In the classic formulation of this rule, Lord Alverstone stated in *West Rand Central Gold Mining Co* v *R* (1905) that custom "will be acknowledged and applied by our municipal tribunals when legitimate occasion arises" – adding the major caveat that the custom must be clearly shown to exist and not be a mere figment of scholarly imaginings.

The current position appears to be that custom, clearly established, will be accepted as part of the law of the land except in the face of a contrary statute or decision of a higher court: *Chung Chi Cheung* v *The King* (1939); *Thakrar* v *Home Secretary* (1974); *Trendtex Trading Corporation* v *Central Bank of Nigeria* (1977); *Ex Parte Pinochet (No 1)* (2000).

In *Lord Advocate's Reference No 1 of 2000* (2001), the High Court of Justiciary stated that a "rule of customary international law is a rule of Scots law", presumably subject to the same qualifications as apply south of the Border. The court emphasised that custom was not foreign law and was therefore deemed to be within judicial knowledge; and that a Scottish court could look to a variety of written sources for evidence of the custom, particularly evidence of *opinion juris*.

The case of *Mortensen* v *Peters* (1906) is perhaps the most important Scottish case on international law. An appeal against conviction for illegal fishing 3 miles from the coast of the Moray Firth by the Danish master of a Norwegian fishing boat claimed that the area, designated in a by-law under the Herring Fishery (Scotland) Act 1889, was, under customary international law, outside the jurisdiction of the Scottish courts. The High Court rejected the appeal, holding that the "presumption" that the custom was part of Scots law had been displaced by the clear language of the statute. Subsequently, following protests by foreign Governments, it was acknowledged that the decision was inconsistent with international law, prosecutions against foreign vessels were suspended; and the 1889 Act was replaced by a statute of 1909 in conformity with international law.

The United States

As it falls to each States to determine for itself the effect to be given to treaties and custom within its legal system, practice throughout the world varies, and the monism and dualism theories become nothing more than rough descriptions of what States provide in their constitutional arrangements. Most accounts of that practice, properly the subject of constitutional and not international law, include reference to the position in the United States.

Because Art VI of the US Constitution declares treaties to be the supreme law of the land, and because the Senate is involved in the ratification of treaties, the US permits some treaties to have effect in municipal law without legislative intervention: *Foster & Elam* v *Neilson* (1829). The criteria for any particular treaty provision being self-executing are that it must be capable, standing alone, of creating right and duties enforceable in the courts; in other words, it must be legally perfect in itself, containing no elements of uncertainty, ambiguity or futurity.

In relation to custom, the US inherited from colonial times the rule that custom is automatically part of US (federal) law. This proposition is vouched by the Supreme Court decision in *The Paquete Habana* (1900), a decision remarkable also for the lengths the court went to in order to demonstrate the existence of the custom in issue. The rule is qualified, as in the UK, to the extent that automatic incorporation will not occur in the face of a contrary federal statute or decision of a higher court.

Essential Facts

- A State's constitution determines whether a rule of international law is part of its municipal law.
- In the UK, treaties are not part of the law without specific incorporation by legislation.
- Custom is automatically part of UK law unless contrary to legislation or the decision of a higher court.

Essential Cases

The Parlement Belge (1879): even though a Convention had been concluded in 1876 giving immunity in English courts to Belgian mail ships, that Convention could not be invoked to give immunity to the *Parlement Belge*, a Belgian mail packet involved in a collision with an English steam-tug, because there had been no legislation making the Convention part of English law.

Mortensen v Peters (1906): a Scottish court held that a Danish fisherman could be prosecuted for fishing illegally in an area designated in a by-law under an Act of Parliament even though the area was, under customary international law, high sea and open to fishing by all.

4 SUBJECTS OF INTERNATIONAL LAW

INTERNATIONAL PERSONALITY

Legal persons in any legal system are those with rights and duties and the capacity to enforce these rights. International law recognises personality primarily in States, but also to a lesser extent in international organisations and individuals; and, to an even lesser extent, in a range of other entities that play some role on the international stage, such as multinational corporations, non-governmental organisations and national liberation movements, often referred to as "non-State actors".

Traditionally, those entities, primarily States, with international rights and duties, and procedural capacity, have been referred to as the subjects of international law. Before the 20th century, States were the only subjects of international law, everything else (individuals, territory, the sea) being objects of international law, meaning things regulated by international law.

Since the mid-20th century, first international organisations, particularly the United Nations, and then individuals, through the human rights movement, came to be recognised as possessing a measure of international personality. They too were international persons, subjects of international law, albeit with fewer rights and duties than States.

Describing an entity as an international person, or a subject of international law, is somewhat meaningless unless one is told what specific rights and duties, and procedural capacity, that entity has. Nonetheless, the concept of international personality, with varied content, has remained the standard method of examining the rights and duties of international actors, not least because it emphasises the traditional and primary role of States in the international legal system.

STATES

The primacy of States in international law is beyond question. Attempts to reformulate international law in terms of different principal actors, usually individuals, are doomed to failure because of the realities of international affairs. International affairs are conducted by States, acting individually or through some organisation they have set up, and international law, being an expression of the rules applicable in international affairs, is the law created by and primarily for States.

Modern international law is created by States, the principal sources being treaties (involving express agreements between States) and custom (involving implicit agreement between States). There is no international legislature competing with States to create international law, and no court creating international common law.

The primacy of States is bolstered by a number of particular rules of international law. Under Art 34 of the Statute of the ICJ, only States may be parties to cases before the court. In relation to the diplomatic protection of individuals and companies for injuries they may have suffered at the hands of another State, it is only the State of which the individual or company is a national that can act. And when it so acts, it is asserting its own right, and not acting as some kind of agent for the individual or company: *Mavrommatis Palestine Concession Case* (1924).

In the *Reparations Opinion* (1949), the International Court stated that "a State possesses the totality of international rights and duties recognized by international law". It is clear from this landmark opinion what the Court thought were the important elements that went into international personality: treaty-making power, privileges and immunities and the capacity to bring an international claim.

States have a general and unrestricted treaty-making power. In fact, the Vienna Convention on the Law of Treaties of 1969 defines treaties exclusively in terms of agreements concluded between States. States enjoy in the territory of other States extensive privileges and immunities (see Chapter 6). While the *Reparations Opinion* recognised the special right of the UN to bring a claim on behalf of its officials, the general rule remains that it is States that are competent to pursue international claims (see Chapter 7.)

In sum, States enjoy full international personality with all its attendant rights and duties. They have that personality *ab initio* and *ipso jure* – from the moment of their birth and by virtue of law.

INTERNATIONAL ORGANISATIONS

International organisations are of fairly recent origin, the first probably being the Rhine Commission established after the 1815 Congress of Vienna among the riparian States to regulate navigation on the river in their common interests. The first global international organisation with a general and far-reaching competence, designed to deal with more than the administrative and technical and to be a forum for the resolution of disputes among great and small States was established as the League of Nations in 1919. Significantly the League had permanent organs and a permanent secretariat. Its successor in 1945, the United Nations, shares the same features, but with some noteworthy differences. The ambit of the UN is even more extensive than the League, extending into the social and economic fields. The weaknesses of the League's arrangements for peace and security are to some extent remedied by a more centralised system based on the Security Council (see Chapter 8). Also, voting in the major organs of the UN are changed from unanimity to majority, although the Security Council retains a veto in the five major powers.

Thus, from 1945, there was an actor on the international stage that had extensive competences and responsibilities; and an actor not wholly dependent on the unanimous agreement of its members. The issue of the status under international law of this new actor did not take long to arise.

In the late 1940s, some UN personnel in Palestine had been killed and others injured by the activities of Jewish groups seeking to establish a State of Israel. The General Assembly asked the ICJ for an advisory opinion as to whether the UN could make a claim against the responsible Government (by this time the Government of Israel) for the deaths and injuries suffered by its personnel. In the *Reparations Opinion* (1949), the ICJ advised that the UN had the capacity to make a claim in respect of the harm to its officials.

The ICJ held that the UN had international personality, deducing personality from the facts that the Charter gave the UN the power to conclude treaties and accorded it privileges and immunities. It added that the UN was "at present the supreme type of international organisation, and it could not carry out the intentions of its founders if it was devoid of international personality". Accordingly, it had "a large measure of international personality and the capacity to operate on the international plane".

The Court emphasised that the UN was not a State and that its international personality was not the same as that of a State. It then went on to articulate how one would identify the rights and duties of the UN – and indeed any other international organisation: they "depend upon its powers and functions as specified or implied in its constituent documents and developed in practice".

The international personality of the UN is objective in the sense that it is applicable against all States, members or not, an important holding in this opinion as the UN was seeking to make a claim against a non-Member State, Israel. As the Court said, "fifty States, representing the vast majority of the members of the international community, had the power, in conformity with international law, to bring into being an entity possessing objective international personality, and not merely personality recognized by them alone".

Other international organisations have subjective personality, that is personality *vis-à-vis* their members. Beyond members, these organisations will have such aspects of personality as non-members are prepared to accept. A State that concludes a treaty with the EU cannot then deny the legal existence of the EU or its power to conclude treaties, and must observe the terms of the treaty in the same way as it would with any other international person.

While the international personality of States is original in the sense that it is an inherent attribute of Statehood, the personality of international organisations is derivative. Using the ICJ's analysis, the powers and functions contained in constituent instruments are nothing more than those granted by States; and the powers and functions developed in practice are nothing more than those tolerated by States. International organisations have no independent existence apart from States. Whatever international rights and duties they have, they have by derivation from States.

INDIVIDUALS

Similarly, where individuals, or groups of individuals, have rights and duties under international law, they too have them by derivation from States.

Up to the middle of the last century, it was common to regard individuals as objects, rather than subjects, of international law. They were susceptible to regulation by international law, but they were not thought of the recipients of rights in international law. Where, exceptionally, rights were granted to individuals by treaty, these rights would find their way into municipal law via statute – and the source of the rights would be seen as the statute and not the treaty. An individual injured or harmed by the acts of a foreign State had no redress but through his or her own Government.

It had long been recognised that individuals were subject to obligations arising out of international law. Since the 18th century, piracy was accepted as an international crime; and, more than that, the pirate, as an enemy of all humankind (*hostis humani generis*), was subject to seizure on the high seas, prosecution and punishment by any State. Beginning in the 19th century, Conventions were adopted for the identification of war crimes and the punishment of war criminals.

All that changed in the immediate aftermath of World War II. According to Art 2(3) of the Charter, one of the four broad purposes of the UN is "promoting and encouraging respect for human rights and for fundamental freedoms for all without distinction as to race, sex, language, or religion". The promotion of human rights resulted in a multiplicity of global and regional instruments (see Chapter 9). Individuals began to have rights under international law, rights that they could invoke against their own Governments.

At the same time, the work of the International Military Tribunal, sitting in Nuremberg to try the major German war criminals, firmly established the principle that individuals could be criminally liable for war crimes and crimes against humanity, including genocide. In its judgment, the IMT said:

> "Crimes against international law are committed by men, not by abstract entities, and only by punishing individuals who commit such crimes can the provisions of international law be enforced."

It is from the twin areas of human rights and international criminal law that individuals have now emerged as clear subjects of international law. That cannot be denied. However, it has to be accepted that individuals have only such rights, and are exposed to such obligations, as States chose; and, apart from those few human right treaties which give them a right to pursue a remedy before an international tribunal, individuals have no procedural capacity.

Essential Facts

- States are the prime – and were at one time the sole – subjects of international law (or international persons).
- International organisations have such international personality as is accorded to them by States in their constituent documents and as developed in practice.
- Individuals have limited rights under international law, and even more limited procedural capacity, accorded to them by States.

Essential Case

Reparations Opinion (1949): the ICJ ruled that the UN had international personality, in particular the right to make an international claim against a State, through the UN Charter implicitly and explicitly in its treaty-making power and its privileges and immunities.

5 STATES: BIRTH TO DEATH

STATEHOOD

Criteria of statehood

Statehood is the state of being a State. The conditions of statehood are accepted as being set out in Art 1 of the Montevideo Convention on the Rights and Duties of States of 1933:

> "The state as a person of international law should possess the following qualifications: (a) a permanent population; (b) a defined territory; (c) government; and (d) capacity to enter into relations with the other states."

These criteria were endorsed by the Badinter Arbitration Commission, established to resolve legal issues arising out of the break-up of Yugoslavia, in *Opinion No 1* (1992), describing a State as "a community which consists of a territory and a population subject to an organized political authority."

While Art 1(a)–(c) of the Montevideo Convention appears to cover essentially factual matters, they are not completely free from difficulty. At one time, there was concern that some States were too small in population to enable them to fulfill the obligations required by some constituent treaties. When Liechtenstein sought admission to the League of Nations in 1920, it was refused, not because it was not a State, but because it was too small to carry out its obligations under the Covenant. The UN has no particular regard to the size of the population of a new member. Nauru, with a population of 9,300 at its last census (and a territory of 21 square kilometres), became an independent State in 1968 and a UN member in 1999.

It is axiomatic that a State must have some territory, but, as with Nauru, the amount does not seem important. The Montevideo Convention requires a "defined" territory, but there is no requirement in the practice of States that the borders be definitively settled. Israel became a State in 1948 with disputed borders – and its borders have continued to be disputed since. Estonia became independent in 1991 on the break-up of the Soviet Union even though its eastern borders with Russia were in dispute. On borders, the ICJ has said that "there is no rule that the land frontiers of a State must be fully delimited and defined, and often in various places and for long periods they are not": *North Sea Continental Shelf Cases* (1969).

It is equally axiomatic that a State must have, in the words of the Convention, "government" – not "a government" – implying that there must be some coherent political structure effectively governing a territory and people; the precise form of that political structure is not important. In the *Aaland Islands Case* (1920), an international committee of jurists, trying to identify precisely when Finland became an independent State, said:

> "This certainly did not take place until a stable political organisation had been created, and until the public authorities had become strong enough to assert themselves throughout the territory of the state …"

And in *Opinion No 1* (1992), the Badinter Arbitration Commission thought that the "the form of internal political organisation and the constitutional provisions" were not as important as "the government's sway over the population and the territory".

More problematic is the requirement for statehood that there be a capacity to enter relations with other States. This capacity involves more than the empty shell of a Ministry of Foreign Affairs within a Government with which no other State will have dealings. It requires independent action on the international plane – and is therefore related to the question of recognition. To satisfy the conditions of statehood, a State must be able to interact with other States, and an entity that cannot interact with other States because these other States will not interact with it is not a State.

In the years between 1965 and 1979, the former British colony of Southern Rhodesia had a permanent population within a defined territory under an effective Government, yet it was not strictly a State because it was not recognised by any State, not even its neighbour, apartheid-era South Africa. Similarly, the four Bantustans created in South Africa between 1976 and 1981 as black African homelands and intended as States were recognised by no State other than their creator and were consequently not States under international law.

Loss of statehood

An existing State does not lose its statehood because it loses some population or some territory; nor because its Government surrenders some of its functions to the Government of another State; nor because it loses some of its capacity to interact with other States. Somalia remains a State despite the fact that it has had no effective Government for nearly two decades. Statehood, once attained, can only be lost through the complete extinction of the State, as in its absorption into another State, or complete alienation of its independence. When, in 1931, Austria proposed entering a customs union with Germany, the PCIJ held that it would not thereby cease to be a State as long as it maintained "its own government and administration ... within her own frontiers": *Austro–German Customs Union Case* (1931).

Indeed, the more usual phenomenon is now the emergence of new States rather than the disappearance of existing States, though the two are related. The disintegration of the Soviet Union in the early 1990s led to the extinction of the USSR as a State and the emergence of 15 new States in its place, including Russia as the successor of the USSR. In 1993, Czechoslovakia was peacefully dismantled and replaced by the Czech Republic and Slovakia. Since the early 1990s, the Socialist Federal Republic of Yugoslavia gradually dismantled itself into six new States (seven if Kosovo is added).

The Badinter Arbitration Commission considered that the question of the extinction of the Socialist Federal Republic of Yugoslavia was a factual matter to be determined according to the established criteria for statehood: *Opinion No 1* (1992). In *Opinion No 8* (1992), the Commission, having regard to the complete disappearance of the federal governmental institutions and the assumption of sovereign authority over the former federal territory and population by the various component States of the federation, concluded that the SFRY no longer existed as a State.

SELF-DETERMINATION

Emergence of the principle

The days are long gone when a new State might come into existence from the settlement of a people on vacant territory and the creation of some governmental structure with a capacity to deal with other States. Today, new States arise out of the dismantling of old States or the emergence of a people from colonialism, foreign occupation or alien domination through the exercise of the right of self-determination.

The right of self-determination is of relatively recent origin. In the *Aaland Islands Case* (1920), an international committee of jurists considered that self-determination, while an important political principle, had not attained the status of a "positive rule of the Law of Nations", not least because it was not mentioned in the Covenant of the League of Nations.

Self-determination is mentioned in the UN Charter (Arts 1(2) and 55) as one of the goals of the UN. The General Assembly's Declaration on the Granting of Independence to Colonial Countries and Peoples of 1960 provides in para 2:

> "All peoples have the right to self-determination; by virtue of that right they freely determine their political status and freely pursue their economic, social and cultural development."

This same statement appears as common Art 1 of the International Covenants on Civil and Political Rights and on Economic, Social and Cultural Rights of 1966, in the authoritative Friendly Relations Declaration of 1970, and is repeated in series of General Assembly resolutions. In the *Namibia Opinion* (1971), in interpreting the term "sacred trust" as the standard of treatment to which Namibia was entitled, the ICJ considered that it could not ignore developments in the law relating to self-determination.

The Court, in the *Western Sahara Case* (1975), was prepared to hold that self-determination trumped claims that Morocco and Mauritania might have over the territory under traditional customary rules on acquiring title to territory, implying that the principle had the status of a peremptory norm of general international law from which no derogation is possible (*jus cogens*). In the *East Timor Case* (1995), the ICJ described self-determination as "one of the essential principles of contemporary international law". The Badinter Arbitration Commission expressly considered self-determination to be a peremptory norm: *Opinion No 1* (1992). There is now no dispute but that the principle of self-determination constitutes not only a rule of customary law, but also a *jus cogens* norm.

The who of self-determination

The General Assembly's 1960 resolution, from its title and its preamble, is clearly intended for the benefit of colonial peoples. Yet, the language used extends beyond colonial peoples; para 2 refers to "all peoples" and para 1 condemns "alien subjugation, domination and exploitation". To whom, beyond those in colonies, does the right apply? The Quebecois? The Basque separatists? The Scots?

At one time, it was thought that distinctiveness of race, language, religion or culture was an important factor in identifying those entitled to self-determination. After all, colonial peoples were invariable of a different race, language and culture from their colonial masters. The Aaland Islanders, whose right to self-determination was at issue in 1920, were of a different race and culture from the Finns, whose country was claiming the islands.

While distinctiveness may be one factor in identifying a people, it is not the critical factor. In a compelling exposition of the relevant international law, the Supreme Court of Canada, admitting that the definition of a people "remains somewhat uncertain", did not think that the common language and culture shared by the Quebecois was important in deciding whether they had a right to self-determination: *Reference re Secession of Quebec* (1998). Viewing colonial peoples as the intended and primary recipients of the right of self-determination, the Supreme Court decided that the right extended to other peoples who "were blocked from a meaningful exercise of [the] right to self-determination internally" – in other words, blocked from participation in the governance of their own country. As a consequence, the Quebecois, having full and equal rights of participation and involvement in provincial and federal affairs, did not have a right to self-determination in the sense of entitling them to secede from the Canadian federation.

In this, the Canadian Supreme Court drew a distinction between internal and external self-determination. The former is the right to participation and involvement in a country's governance; the latter is the right to independence as a sovereign State. On this analysis, the former is a right that should be available to all people within the territory of a State; the latter is available only to colonial peoples and to those who are consistently denied a meaningful role in their own governance. In the words of the Court, external self-determination is therefore limited to:

> "situations of former colonies; where a people is oppressed, as for example under foreign domination; or where a definable group is denied meaningful access to government to pursue their political, economic, social and cultural development".

The how of self-determination

How are a people seeking to exercise a right to self-determination to "freely determine" their political status and development? In the *Western Sahara Case*, the Court talked of the "freely expressed will of the peoples". There may be no formal requirement to hold a referendum or plebiscite, but those asserting the right have to demonstrate some concerted desire on the part of the population to change the status quo.

The what of self-determination

The essence of the right of self-determination is that a qualifying people decide for themselves what their political future should be. The 1960

General Assembly resolution was silent on what the range of options might be, but the 1970 Friendly Relations Declaration specified the possible outcomes:

> The establishment of a sovereign and independent State, the free association or integration with an independent State or the emergence into any other political status freely determined by a people ..."

This range of options is clearly appropriate for those entitled to external self-determination. As for those entitled to, but not getting, internal self-determination, these outcomes are not generally available. For them, secession is not available. Just as self-determination is a peremptory norm of international law, so the territorial integrity of States is a long-standing, fundamental principle of international law. The 1960 General Assembly resolution (in para 6) subordinates the right of self-determination to the "national unity and the territorial integrity of a country". The *Quebec* case acknowledged this tension, holding that territorial integrity must prevail save "in the exceptional situation of an oppressed or colonial people". The Badinter Commission's *Opinion No 2* (1992) stated:

> "It is well established that, whatever the circumstances, the right to self-determination must not involve any changes to existing frontiers at the time of independence ..."

In sum, the right of self-determination applies to everyone. It is a peremptory norm of general international law. In normal circumstances, the right is satisfied for all people by their participation and involvement in their own governance. Where a group within an existing State is denied a meaningful role in government, it can do no more than assert its right. There is no right in that group to secede and form a new State, except, possibly, where the right is consistently and persistently denied. A colonial people is entitled to full external self-determination, which would include the possibility of sovereign independence.

The *Kosovo Unilateral Declaration of Independence Opinion*, presently before the ICJ, in which the it has been asked whether the 2008 declaration of sovereign independence by the Provisional Institutions of Self-Government of Kosovo is compatible with international law, can hardly depart from the current clear understanding that secession is impermissible except in colonial and other egregious circumstances; and, in the Kosovan situation, reversion to the autonomous status of the province within Serbia would satisfy internal self-determination.

RECOGNITION

Nature of recognition

As a term of art in international law, recognition denotes the acknowledgement and acceptance by a State of the existence of a newly emergent State or of a new Government emerging irregularly in an existing State. Through recognition, a State indicates its willingness to deal with the new entity on the international plane and to accept certain rights and privileges and immunities for the new entity in its municipal law.

There has been debate about whether recognition is constitutive or declaratory – whether recognition itself constitutes the new entity as a State or whether recognition merely acknowledges the existence of a new State and the attendant consequences. The Montevideo Convention of 1933 expressly provides (in Art 3) that the political existence of a State is independent of recognition; and that declaratory view of recognition is supported by State practice. If a State exists from the time it satisfies the criteria of statehood, and recognition is nothing more than an acknowledgement of that fact, with whom can a totally un-recognised State interact? With whom did the self-declared State of Rhodesia interact between 1965 and 1979? A State may well have political existence without any recognition, but, if it is to have any relations with other States, recognition is necessary.

Recognition of States and Governments

It is useful to draw a distinction between the recognition of States and of Governments. Any new State emerging in accordance with the criteria set out in the Montevideo Convention or – much more likely today – emerging from decolonisation or the fragmentation of an existing State will require recognition by other States if it is to be a full member of the international community.

The emergence of a new Government in an existing State through some normal constitutional process, like a general election, does not require recognition: the new Government will simply step into the shoes of the previous Government. But where the process is abnormal or unconstitutional, as in a *coup d'état* or revolution, recognition is required before the new Government will be regarded as representing its State. The change from the Bush to the Obama administrations after the November 2008 US General Election did not call for recognition; the installation of the Augusto Pinochet regime following the forcible overthrow of the constitutionally elected Government of Salvador Allende in 1973 Chile, being unconstitutional, called for recognition.

Recognition criteria

Recognition is a unilateral, voluntary and political act. At one time, States employed a wide range of political factors in deciding whether or not to grant recognition, sometimes using the withholding of recognition as a mark of disapproval. The practice of States clearly establishes that there is no legal duty to recognise a new State or Government; compare Hersch Lauterpacht's argument in his *Recognition in International Law* (1947) that there is such a duty if the criteria for recognition are satisfied.

Increasingly over the years, States have come to appreciate the importance, not least for diplomatic and trade reasons, of accepting factual situations and, therefore, of recognising regimes, however odious, if they are in effective control. In *Opinion No 1* (1992), the Badinter Arbitration Commission emphasised both the voluntary nature of recognition and the important link between recognition and "reality".

The criteria for recognition have coalesced around a number of principles. In relation to the recognition of States, these principles are the tests set out in the Montevideo Convention, with the addition that, in relation to the requirement that there be "government", that government must be both effective and durable. For the recognition of new Governments, these principles are effective authority over the population and territory, coupled with a real likelihood of continuation, often described as stability.

These recognition criteria are, of course, open to interpretation, allowing existing States flexibility in their appreciation of whether an emergent State or Government satisfies the criteria. Further political flexibility arises in the timing of recognition. The US recognised the State (and Government) of Israel *de facto* on 14 May 1948, the very day on which the Provisional Government of Israel proclaimed a new State of Israel. The US recognised the Soviet Union on 16 November 1933, 16 years after the USSR came into existence.

Over the years, various attempts have been made to introduce further criteria into recognition. In 1932, US Secretary of State Henry L Stimson declared that the US would not recognise territorial changes executed by force, applying his doctrine to the Japanese seizure of Manchuria; the doctrine was invoked in 1940 in relation to the Soviet annexation of the three Baltic States. In 1991, the European Community promulgated Guidelines on the Recognition of New States in Eastern Europe and the Soviet Union, conditioning recognition by EC Member States on respect for self-determination, the rule of law, democracy, human rights, the rights of minorities and the inviolability of frontiers. These "legitimacy" criteria, set for the emerging States in the disintegrating Yugoslavia and USSR, are evolving into general standards to be used in the recognition of States and Governments.

Recognition *de jure* and *de facto*

Following British practice, a number of States found it useful to recognise a new Government, and exceptionally a new State, as existing *de facto* when there were reservations about some aspect of the new entity and as existing *de jure* when all the criteria required of a new regime were met. The missing ingredient was invariably the likelihood of permanence. The UK recognised the Soviet Government *de facto* in March 1921, three years after the Russian Revolution, and *de jure* in February 1924. The US recognised Israel *de facto* in May 1948 and *de jure* in January 1949.

During the Spanish Civil War, the UK recognised the existing (republican) Government *de jure* and the insurgent (nationalist) authorities *de facto* over the area under their control. Recognising two Governments over the same territory led to the anomalous but predictable result that a UK court was forced into granting immunity to the *de facto* nationalist authorities in an action brought by the *de jure* Government: *The Arantzatzu Mendi* (1939).

Recognition modes

Recognition may be express or implied. The trend is away from express, formal acts of recognition to recognition by implication. As a matter of policy, the UK decided in 1980 that it would replace express recognition of new Governments with "dealings" from whose nature recognition might be implied. The result has been that recognition of Governments *per se* has diminished in importance, throwing an additional burden on the courts. In *Republic of Somalia* v *Woodhouse Drake & Carey Suisse SA* (1993), when considering whether the interim Government of Somalia was entitled to succeed to rights acquired by its predecessor, Hobhouse J said that the issue is "left to be ascertained as a matter of inference"; and, looking at the degree of control exercised by the interim Government, recognition by other States and three letters from the Foreign and Commonwealth Office, he concluded that the interim Government could not succeed to the rights of the former Government.

What dealings, then, imply recognition? It appears that only two dealings categorically imply recognition: the exchange of diplomatic representatives and the conclusion of a treaty on a particular topic. The exchange of diplomatic representatives has become the standard way by which the UK indicates the dealings that lead to the consequences associated with the recognition of Governments. While the conclusion of a bilateral treaty will constitute recognition-sufficient dealings, being a party to a multilateral treaty with an "unrecognised" regime will not.

Collective recognition and non-recognition

Recognition is a unilateral act by States, based upon their appreciation of what criteria are relevant and whether these criteria are satisfied. There is no collective recognition of new States or Governments. Despite the fact that one of the conditions for admission to the UN is that the applicant be a State (Art 4 of the Charter), voting to admit an entity is not tantamount to recognition.

While there may be no collective recognition, there may be collective standards of recognition. The EC's 1991 Guidelines on the Recognition of New States in Eastern Europe and the Soviet Union are intended to set criteria for its Member States in their recognition practice. There may be collective non-recognition. In 1965 and 1966, the Security Council, calling the break-away white minority Government in Southern Rhodesia unlawful, called on all States not to recognise the regime. Similarly, the Security Council in Resolution 276 (1970) called upon States not to recognise the continued presence of South Africa in South West Africa (now Namibia); the International Court declared this obligation to extend to non-members of the UN on the basis that the resolution barred "*erga omnes* the legality of a situation which is maintained in violation of international law": *Namibia Opinion* (1971).

Recognition effects

Internationally, recognition elevates the new entity to the international plane *vis-à-vis* the recognising State. It has long been maintained that, while unrecognised entities are subject to obligations under international law, they do not enjoy all the rights of international law. This begs the question of how many States need to recognise a new entity to allow it access to all international law's rights. As there is no satisfactory answer to that question, the better view is to regard recognition as the trigger for the application of international rules between the recogniser and the recognised.

As to the municipal effects of recognition, there are a number of consequences – and those of UK municipal law are fairly typical. The basic principle was stated by Lord Chancellor Eldon in *City of Berne* v *Bank of England* (1804): "it was extremely difficult to say [that] a judicial Court can take notice of a government, never authorized by the government of the Country in which the Court sits".

Recognition allows a foreign Government to raise an action in the courts of the UK: *City of Berne* (1804). Recognition entitles the Government to sovereign immunity: *The Arantazazu Mendi* (1939). Recognition enables effect to be given in the UK to acts of the Government. So, in *Luther* v *Sagor* (1921), the claim of the plaintiff Russian company to recover timber sold to the defendant company by the Soviet authorities was successful at first instance because, as the USSR was not recognised by the UK, no effect could be given to the decree seizing the timber; in the Court of Appeal, effect was given to the Soviet decree because the USSR was by then recognised by the UK.

The adverse effects of non-recognition can be overcome by the "delegated authority" theory. In *Carl Zeiss Stiftung* v *Rayner and Keeler Ltd (No 2)* (1967), an act of the German Democratic Republic was given effect despite lack of recognition, because the GDR was held to exercise powers delegated by the Soviet Union, recognised by the UK as the *de jure* Government of East Germany. In *Gur Corporation* v *Trust Bank of Africa Ltd* (1987), the Court of Appeal applied the concept of "delegated authority" in allowing *locus standi* to the unrecognised Republic of Ciskei.

STATE SUCCESSION

State succession occurs when the whole or part of the territory of one State falls under the sovereign authority of another State; and the rules of State succession are designed to regulate the consequences of that change in relation to existing treaties, public property and public debts. In a masterly summary, the Badinter Arbitration Commission stated in *Opinion No 1* (1992):

> "'State succession' means the replacement of one State by another in the responsibility for the international relations of territory. This occurs whenever there is a change in the territory of the State. The phenomenon of State succession is governed by the principles of international law, from which the Vienna Conventions of 23 August 1978 and 8 April 1983 have drawn inspiration. In compliance with these principles, the outcome of succession should be equitable, the States concerned being free to settle terms and conditions by agreement."

The rules of State succession are uncertain and controversial, though *Opinion No 1* identified the two cardinal principles: that succession issues are to be determined by agreement (often called a devolution agreement) between the predecessor State and the successor State; and that the agreed arrangements, whatever they may be, are to be equitable.

Treaties

A Vienna Convention on Succession of States in Respect of Treaties was adopted in 1978, but its influence is minimal as it entered into force only in 1996; it has only 22 States Parties and none of the major powers is a party. Nonetheless, it reinforces the importance of treaty succession being regulated by devolution agreements between the predecessor and successor States. It also provides that newly independent States, essentially meaning States former colonies, should start with a clean slate (*tabula rasa*), leaving them with the choice of which treaties to opt into. In practice, successor States tend to accept all the treaties concluded by the predecessor State, sometimes later seeking some alteration in their terms. There are *dicta* to the effect that, certainly for vital human rights treaties, like the Genocide Convention, succession is automatic: *Application of the Genocide Convention Case* (1996).

Property

The 1983 Vienna Convention on Succession of States in respect of State Property, Archives and Debts has attracted so little support that it has not entered into force. This Convention confirms the basic rule that all public property of the predecessor passes without compensation to the successor, subject to respect for the property rights of individuals and companies. Public archives too pass to the successor.

Real problems arise in relation to military bases, their equipment and personnel. While military bases, as public property, pass to the successor and the predecessor's troops have no right to remain in the successor State, difficult problems arise in relation to sophisticated military equipment. The resolution of these problems can only be by agreement. It took till August 1994, 3 years after Estonia's independence, for agreements to secure the complete withdrawal of Russian troops, tanks and aircraft; and it was only in 1995 that the decommissioning by Russia of the Paldiski nuclear base was completed.

Debts

The 1983 Vienna Convention assumes the long-held understanding that the apportionment of the public debt (and assets) of the predecessor State would be regulated by agreement with the successor State. In relation to newly independent States, such apportionment can only be made to the successor State for debts arising out of some activity on the successor's territory, a rule that one would expect to figure in all devolution agreements.

Succession in international organisations

State succession is not to be confused with succession in international organisations, which occurs when an existing member splits into two or more States. Within the UN, the presumptive rule was established by the partition of India, an original member, in 1947, when India was allowed to retain the Indian seat in the General Assembly and Pakistan was admitted as a new member. Then, when Pakistan itself split into east and west Pakistan in 1974, Pakistan was allowed to retain the Pakistani seat and Bangladesh was admitted as a new member.

On the dissolution of the USSR in 1991, Russia was permitted, with the acquiescence of the former Soviet republics, to retain the USSR's seat in the UN, including the permanent membership (and accompanying veto) in the Security Council. This rule, arising from practice and based on the succession of the largest and most important part of the former Member State, was not followed after the break-up of the Socialist Federal Republic of Yugoslavia. Given that the SFRY had completely disintegrated and that no acceptable rump was left to succeed to its original membership, each of the former States of the SFRY was required to apply for admission as new members. So, Bosnia and Herzegovina, Croatia, and Slovenia were admitted in 1992, the Former Yugoslav Republic of Macedonia in 1993 and the Federal Republic of Yugoslavia (Serbia and Montenegro) in 2000. When the FRY split with the independence of Montenegro in 2006, Serbia, the larger part of that federation, succeeded to the FRY seat under the new name of Serbia, and Montenegro was admitted as a new member.

Essential Facts

- The basic unit of international law, the State, must have a permanent population, defined territory, government and capacity to enter into relations with the other States.
- The right of self-determination applies to all peoples, but allows only colonies and territories persistently denied a role in their own governance to attain sovereign independence.
- Recognition is important internationally in establishing relations between international actors and municipally in conferring rights on the recognised Government. There is increasing concern that recognition should have regard to the legitimacy of the new State or Government.

- The rules on the succession of rights and duties of States are vague, though emphasising that the matter be equitably regulated by agreement.

Essential Cases

Reference re Secession of Quebec (1998): the Supreme Court of Canada held that the people of Quebec, while entitled to and enjoying a role in their own governance, had no right of self-determination so as to entitle them to secede from the Canadian federation.

Opinion No 1 (1992): the Badinter Arbitration Commission ruled that effective government was a critical component of statehood, that self-determination had the elevated status of *jus cogens* and that the rules of State succession required, at a minimum, an equitable agreement between the predecessor and successor States.

Luther v Sagor (1921): in this English decision, it was held that, while the acts of the Soviet Government could not be given effect in British courts before recognition by the UK, after recognition they could.

6 STATES: POWERS AND AUTHORITY

SOVEREIGNTY

Elements

International law and its literature abound with references to sovereignty. Yet, there is no generally accepted definition of the term or its implications in international law. Max Huber, the arbiter in the *Island of Palmas Case* (1928), drew a distinction between internal sovereignty and what he called "political sovereignty", better described as external sovereignty. In its internal aspect, sovereignty encompasses both *dominium* and *imperium*. *Dominium* is the ultimate ownership of all the land territory enclosed within a State's boundaries. It does not matter that the State has, through its legal system, made arrangements for parcels of land to be privately owned; it retains the ultimate title to all its land. *Imperium* is the supreme authority of the Government of a State to make and enforce laws. Sometimes called territorial sovereignty, it is, in Huber's words, "the right to exercise therein, to the exclusion of any other State, the functions of a State". A State can, however, delegate law-making and enforcement to another State or an international organisation. The Member States of the European Community have accorded it the power to enact measures that are directly applicable within their territories; these measures are given effect in the courts of the Member States, subject to oversight by the European Court of Justice.

In its external aspect, described by Huber as "a principle of international law", sovereignty comprises independence of action and equality with other States. Independence of action implies that the Government of a State exclusively conducts its own foreign relations, though this does not mean that a State cannot have its foreign relations conducted by another State. Monaco and San Marino, two tiny European States and UN members, have by agreement arranged for their national defence to be undertaken by France and Italy respectively.

The equality component of sovereignty is juridical equality among States. While there may be enormous disparities in wealth, military power and political clout, in law, all States are equal. The UN is based on "the sovereign equality of all its Members" (Charter, Art 2(1)). However, the UN Charter recognises political reality in an organisation designed to maintain international peace and security and applies the Orwellian principle that, while all States are equal, some are more equal than others. So, under Arts 23(1) and 27(3), the five major powers were accorded permanent membership of the Security Council and a veto in substantive votes.

Limitations

Whatever sovereignty means, it does not mean complete and unfettered freedom of action on the international plane. A State enjoys its external sovereignty subject to the rules of international law. Almost every treaty and many rules of customary law to some extent limit States' freedom of action. For example, a State cannot undertake extraordinary rendition, the transportation of terrorist suspects to countries where interrogation techniques amounting to torture are tolerated, because it is a breach of international law under the Torture Convention of 1984 and therefore prohibited.

In the *Wimbledon Case* (1923), Germany's neutrality regulations during the Polish–Soviet war of 1919–21 – expressions of its internal sovereignty – were trumped by Art 380 of the Treaty of Versailles of 1919 guaranteeing unimpeded access to the Kiel Canal for all ships, even the *Wimbledon*, a British-registered vessel carrying military *matériel* to Poland. By virtue of Art 380, the Kiel Canal, wholly located within the territory of Germany, had "ceased to be an internal and national navigable waterway".

TERRITORY

Territory is an essential prerequisite to statehood; and ownership of, and jurisdiction over, territory are necessary concomitants of sovereignty. It is "the space within which the State exercises its supreme authority": *Island of Palmas Case* (1928). However tempting it might be to think that, as there is no vacant territory in the world awaiting claims by States, the traditional rules on acquiring title to territory are now irrelevant, there remain disputes as to boundaries, the resolution of which depends upon the rules by which title may be acquired.

Boundaries

There is no specific corpus of international law for delimiting boundaries, though there are rules of thumb. Ideally, a land boundary should be easy to identify and difficult to cross: *Alaska Boundary Arbitration* (1903). Thus, the watershed of a mountain range may be adopted as an international boundary. If a river is to be the boundary, the precise delineation of that boundary may be the middle of the navigable channel (called the *thalweg*) for a navigable river and the middle of the stream for a non-navigable river.

Another rule of thumb, the principle of *uti possidetis*, has become a rule of international law, transforming colonial administrative boundaries in Latin America, and later Africa, into international boundaries. As the ICJ said in the *Burkina Faso/Mali Frontier Dispute Case* (1986):

> "The essence of the principle lies in its primary aim of securing respect for the territorial boundaries at the moment when independence is achieved. Such territorial boundaries might be no more than delimitation between different administrative divisions or colonies all subject to the same sovereign. In that case, the application of the principle of *uti possidetis* resulted in administrative boundaries being transformed into international frontiers in the full sense of the term."

Uti possidetis has an application beyond the purely colonial context and was considered in relation to the break-up of the USSR and Yugoslavia (see, for example, *Opinions Nos 2 and 3* of the Badinter Arbitration Commission (1992)).

TERRITORIAL ACQUISITION

There are five traditional methods by which title to territory may be acquired.

Occupation

Original title to territory may be acquired by occupation (in Latin, *occupatio*), which requires that the territory in question must be *terra nullius* and that the occupying State must exercise over the territory open, peaceful, continuous and effective governmental authority for a substantial period of time. The *terra nullius* requirement mandates that there be no former or existing sovereign for the territory; it must belong to no-one. The Western Sahara was, prior to Spanish colonisation in 1884, "inhabited by tribes or peoples having a social and political organisation" and was therefore not *terra nullius*: *Western Sahara Case* (1975).

What is required by the exercise of effective governmental authority depends on two factors, described in the *Island of Palmas Case* (1928) as "conditions of time and place". One is inter-temporal law, a doctrine requiring that "a juridical fact must be appreciated in the light of the law contemporary with it": *Island of Palmas Case*. In other words, to exercise governmental authority sufficient to acquire title by occupation, a State must do what was typical of governmental authority at each stage of its occupation. At a time when Governments did little within their own territory but maintain law and order and provide basic services, replicating these for territories being acquired by occupation is sufficient; when Governments came to do more within their own territories, more is required of them for territories being acquired by occupation.

The other factor relates to the circumstances of the territory. Where the territory is well settled, there must be an exercise of governmental authority similar to that in a State's own territory. But when the territory is "thinly populated or unsettled", as Eastern Greenland was in the early 1930s, "very little in the way of the actual exercise of sovereign rights" is required to secure title: *Eastern Greenland Case* (1933). Indeed, in the *Clipperton Island Case* (1931), such was the hostile nature of this tiny coral atoll's environment that title was awarded to France on the basis of its published proclamation of annexation; neither France nor Mexico having effectively settled the island, the French claim was regarded as sufficient to acquire title.

Discovery alone will not give title. Discovery gives an "inchoate" title, a title that must be followed by the effective exercise of governmental authority. In the *Island of Palmas Case*, Spanish discovery of the island and later cession to the US was held insufficient to confer title in the face of effective occupation by the Netherlands.

The requirements for title by occupation are stated by the arbitral tribunal in the *Eritrea/Yemen Case* (1998) to be "the intentional display of power and authority over the territory, by the exercise of jurisdiction and State functions, on a continuous and peaceful basis".

Where two States are contesting title to the same territory, the State which has exercised more governmental authority will prevail. Thus, in the *Minquiers and Ecrehos Case* (1953), where both the UK and France claimed the two island groups in the Channel Islands area, the ICJ, weighing the cases of the two claimants, unanimously concluded that the UK had done more and for longer.

In determining title by occupation, particular importance attaches to the critical date, the date at which the claim is to be determined. It is the date at which any dispute about title crystallises. Acts and events before the critical date are entirely relevant in determining title; acts and events after that date are wholly irrelevant. The critical date in the *Island of Palmas Case* was 1898, the date of the cession of the island to the US at the end of the Spanish–American War; and in the *Western Sahara Case* (1975), it was 1884, the date of Spanish colonisation of the territory.

Acquisitive prescription

Where occupation is not available as a method of acquiring title, because the territory is not *terra nullius*, the process of acquisitive prescription may be utilised. Prescription may also cure defects in a title. In essence, the requirements for prescriptive title are identical to those for title by occupation – the effective exercise of governmental authority.

While scholars have long seen a clear distinction between occupation and prescription, international courts and tribunals have shied away from articulating prescription as a basis for title to territory. In its longest judgment to date, the *Maritime Delimitation and Territorial Questions between Qatar and Bahrain* (2001), the ICJ spoke of consolation of title to territory, rather than occupation or prescription, and used as *indicia* of that consolidation what it called *effectivités*, the facts and circumstances from which it could consolidate sovereignty in one or other of the disputing States. However, in the *Kasikili/Sedudu Island Case* (1999), the Court, accepting that prescription might be the basis of a territorial claim, nonetheless rejected Namibia's prescriptive claim to the island, finding that, while the Masubia tribe of the Caprivi Strip in Namibia used the island for many years, it did so intermittently and for exclusively agricultural purposes, without it being established that the tribe occupied the island *à titre de souverain*.

In the era of colonial expansion and competition of the 18th and 19th centuries, questions arose as to how extensively a State might claim as territory acquired by occupation or prescription. According to one theory, that of continuity, a State could claim territory geographically or topographically adjacent and related to the area over which governmental authority was exercised. Thus, a State with a settlement on a coast would claim inland to the nearest mountain range and along the coast to the nearest river. According to another related theory, that of contiguity, a State could claim territory geographically closer to it than to other States. As occupation and prescription are premised on effective control, claims over territory in which absolutely no State activity in undertaken lack legal foundation. In the *Island of Palmas Case* (1928), Max Huber stated that contiguity was "inadmissible as a legal method of deciding questions of territorial sovereignty, for it is wholly lacking in precision and would in its application lead to arbitrary results".

Contiguity was invoked in the first half of the 20th century by States with territory near (well, hundreds of miles near) Antarctica to make "sector claims" to areas of Antarctica, pie-slice claims on Antarctica defined by the meridians of longitude from the extremities of their territories to the South Pole. Argentina, Chile, Australia and New Zealand made claims from their land territory, France, Norway and the UK from island colonies in the South Atlantic and Pacific Oceans. Some of the claims, as between Chile, Argentina and the UK, overlapped. What little validity these claims ever had came from the mutual recognition of the claimants. Article IV of the Antarctic Treaty of 1959 had the effect of freezing all existing claims to Antarctic territory, while the treaty as a whole regulated activities in Antarctica. The Arctic, being essentially frozen high seas, is incapable of appropriation by any State; however, with climate change making access to the Arctic's hydrocarbon resources, some of the bordering States are invoking the sector principle as part of their argument for extensive continental shelf rights in the area (see Chapter 11).

Cession

It has always been possible for a State to transfer territory to another State. At one time, cession of territory was the price to be paid for losing a war. By Art IV of the Treaty of Utrecht of 1713, ending the War of Spanish Succession (1701–14), Spain ceded Gibraltar to Great Britain. By Art III of the Treaty of Nanjing of 1842, ending the First Opium War, China ceded Hong Kong in perpetuity to Great Britain. The Treaty of Versailles of 1919, ending World War I, made substantial territorial changes in Europe and in the colonies of the vanquished. Largely because of the desire to maintain stability in territorial adjustments made in peace treaties, these treaties are exempt from the normal rule that any treaty concluded under force or coercion is void.

Cession may be the result of a sale of territory, the largest purchaser of territory being the United States. By the Louisiana Purchase of 1803, the US acquired 828,800 square miles of territory from France for a total of $15 million; by the Alaskan Purchase of 1867, the US acquired 586,412 square miles from the Russia for $7.2 million.

An unusual cession occurred in the acquisition the Orkney and Shetland Islands by Scotland in the 15th century. In 1468 and 1469, Christian I of Denmark pledged Orkney and Shetland against the payment of the dowry of his daughter Margaret on her betrothal to James III of Scotland for 50,000 Rhenish guilders and 8,000 Rhenish guilders respectively. That pledge never being redeemed, the two island groups fell to Scotland.

Accretion and avulsion

Changes in territory as a result of the forces of nature are recognised by international law. So, when alluvial deposits at the mouths of river form usable land, that gradual accretion of territory is accorded to the coastal

State. Artificial accretions, as where dykes are erected and land behind the dykes drained to form polders, are equiperated with natural accretions. By avulsion, sudden or violent natural changes, for instance in the course of a river separating two States, will result in a gain of land by one and a loss by the other.

Conquest and subjugation

At one time, conquest and subjugation was a recognised method of acquiring territory. What was necessary was more than simple conquest; the conquering State had to assume the mantle of government of the territory. It might do this through a peace treaty with the vanquished State formally ceding the territory; or it might do this by wielding actual control over the territory *à titre de souverain*.

The prohibition on the use of force in Art 2(4) of the UN Charter, carrying with it the inadmissibility of any gains arising from the illegal use of force, means that territory can no longer be acquired by conquest. In Resolution 242 (1967), and subsequent resolutions, the Security Council has condemned Israel's seizure of territory in the Six-Day War (in the Sinai Peninsula, Gaza Strip, the West Bank, Golan Heights and East Jerusalem) and has called repeatedly for its withdrawal; the preamble to Resolution 242 referred to the "inadmissibility of the acquisition of territory by war". The *Wall Opinion* (2004) confirmed that Israel's rights in the Occupied Territories are not those of a sovereign, but rather of an occupying power under the duties imposed by international humanitarian law. To allow the defensive barrier erected by Israel "would be tantamount to *de facto* annexation".

When Saddam Hussein's forces invaded and conquered Kuwait in August 1990 and immediately annexed Kuwait as Iraq's 19th province, the Security Council in Resolution 662 (1990) declared the annexation to be of "no legal validity" and "null and void".

The Charter prohibition on using force is not retroactive and therefore does not invalidate pre-1945 territorial acquisitions by conquest.

JURISDICTION

In normal parlance, jurisdiction means legal authority. As an aspect of territorial sovereignty, jurisdiction includes the legislative power (to prescribe or proscribe conduct by legislation) and the enforcement power (to compel obedience to the laws of conduct through courts). A State has complete and exclusive legislative authority, except when, in the exercise of its territorial sovereignty, it has surrendered that authority to another

State or to an international organisation. When it comes to enforcing rules of conduct, in particular its own criminal law, States have extensive enforcement authority. The (wafer-thin) majority in the *Lotus Case* (1927), so wrong in so much, was surely right when it said that international law accords States:

> "a wide measure of discretion which is only limited in certain cases by prohibitive rules; as regards other cases, every State remains free to adopt the principles which it regards as best and most suitable. ... [All] that can be required of a State is that it should not overstep the limits which international law places upon its jurisdiction; within these limits, its title to exercise jurisdiction rests in its sovereignty".

In a bold attempt to codify the law on the criminal jurisdiction of States, a Harvard Research team in 1935 identified five principles that States have used to found criminal jurisdiction in their courts. The interplay of these principles can result in more than one State having, and seeking to exercise, jurisdiction over the same person for the same offence. For example, in the *Lotus Case*, the French officer charged with manslaughter after the collision on the high seas of his vessel with a Turkish boat, killing eight Turkish citizens, was subject to trial in France and Turkey. In such a case, the practice is that the State with custody of the alleged offender has the primary right to prosecute. To obviate the risk of that person being subjected to a second prosecution for the same offence in another State with jurisdiction, most States have in place, and international human rights law acknowledges, a prohibition on double jeopardy.

Territoriality

Territoriality locates jurisdiction in the State in whose territory an offence is committed. It is by far the most common principle used by States. The Harvard Research team thought it was "too well established to require an extended discussion of authorities". It is jurisdiction over any crime committed within a State's territory by anyone, national or alien, with the sole exception of those entitled to some form of immunity (see "State immunity" and "Diplomatic immunity", below). For jurisdictional purposes, ships flying the flag of a State and aircraft registered in a State are regarded as subject to that State's jurisdiction.

For transnational crimes, crimes transcending national boundaries, or continuing crimes, crimes begun in one State and completed in another, States employ a subjective territorial principle or an objective territorial principle. The former locates jurisdiction in the State in which a crime is commenced, even though it is consummated in another State; the latter locates jurisdiction in the State in which the crime is consummated, even though it is commenced abroad. The objective territorial principle (and to a lesser extent the security principle) find expression in the practice of some States in the "effects" doctrine, whereby States assume jurisdiction over acts committed abroad on the basis of the deleterious effect they have on and in those States. The use of the effects doctrine, particularly by the United States and particularly in enforcing its anti-trust laws, has proved controversial, opponents arguing that it over-reaches in applying US law to companies abroad with the most minimal connection to the US. In the *Wood Pulp Case* (1988), the European Court of Justice decided that it had jurisdiction over manufacturers with no base in the European Community because the EC was the "place of implementation" of an illegal price-fixing agreement, an application of the objective territorial principle, and not because of any effects doctrine.

While territoriality may be, in the words of the *Lotus Case*, the "fundamental" principle of criminal jurisdiction, "it is not an absolute principle of international law". All the other jurisdictional principles, being subordinate to territoriality, are often described as extra-territorial.

Nationality

The nationality principle of jurisdiction locates jurisdiction in a State for an offence committed by its nationals anywhere. This principle is more commonly used in civilian than common law jurisdictions; and it is invariable restricted to more serious offences. It is, nonetheless, the second most common basis of jurisdiction.

Security

Jurisdiction based on the security (or protective) principle entails prosecution of a non-national for an offence committed abroad. The emphasis here is on the nature of the interest injured rather than the place of the crime or the nationality of the offender. Security jurisdiction is restricted, in the words used by the Harvard Research team, to crimes committed against the "security, territorial integrity or political independence" of the State asserting it.

Passive personality

Related to the security principle, the passive personality principle locates jurisdiction in the State whose nationals are injured by the act of a non-national committed abroad. Little favoured, especially in common law States, it has become more popular of late as part of the Conventions on terrorism (see "Jurisdiction and terrorism", below).

Universality

Much nonsense has been written about universal jurisdiction, jurisdiction in a State over crimes committed anywhere by anyone. In considering universality, the Harvard Research team mentioned only piracy, a pirate being long recognised as *hostis humani generis* (enemy of humankind) and subject to the jurisdiction of any State.

Arguments have been made that universal jurisdiction now extends to war crimes, genocide and crimes against humanity (see Chapter 9), but, for these, the principles of jurisdiction set out in the instruments in which these crimes are declared and defined do not import universality, only a broader application of the existing jurisdictional principles. The debate has been confused by the provisions in some treaties, particularly relating to terrorism (see "Jurisdiction and terrorism", below), that, for certain offences, the custodial State must either prosecute or extradite the alleged offender. Run together serious international crimes, wide jurisdiction to prosecute an alleged offender and, for some crimes, the duty to prosecute or extradite – and the argument becomes that, for serious international crimes, there is not only permissive universal jurisdiction, but mandatory universal jurisdiction.

The Supreme Court of Israel held in *Eichmann* v *Attorney-General* (1962) that the Israel courts had jurisdiction over Adolf Eichmann for his involvement in the Holocaust, crimes committed by a German national outside Israel (indeed at the time when Israel did not exist) "pursuant to the principle of universal jurisdiction". A number of States, including Belgium, Canada, France, Germany and Spain, make provision in their law for universal jurisdiction in their criminal courts over serious international crimes, invariably war crimes, genocide and crimes against humanity. The ICJ has had no occasion to address the question of universal jurisdiction directly. In the *Arrest Warrant Case* (2002), the Court declined to rule on the compatibility with international law of a 1993 Belgian statute conferring universal jurisdiction on the Belgian courts in relation to grave violations of international humanitarian law regardless of where they were committed; it nonetheless declared void an arrest warrant issued by a Belgian court against an incumbent Congolese Foreign Minister, his immunity under international law prevailing over Belgium's assertion of criminal jurisdiction.

Jurisdiction and terrorism

Terrorism has been addressed by the international community piecemeal as a response to particular acts of terrorism. There is no single Convention dealing with terrorism comprehensively, though the UN has been attempting to draft such an instrument for more than a decade. The UN's counter-terrorism regime is in fact 13 Conventions covering such terrorist acts as the hijacking and sabotage of aircraft, hostage-taking, terrorist bombings and nuclear terrorism.

The counter-terrorism regime is predicated on the domestic prosecution of terrorists; from 1963, when the first terrorism Convention was adopted, terrorist crimes have been addressed through each State's criminal justice system. It is because of the existence of this distinct "sectoral regime" for terrorism that the Statute of the International Criminal Court of 1998 does not include terrorism within the Court's jurisdiction (see Chapter 9). The 13 Conventions constituting the terrorism regime share some common features, among which is that each State party is required to make a particular and defined crime part of its criminal law with appropriate penalties; that each State undertakes that it will either prosecute a terrorist suspect in its custody or extradite that suspect (the *aut dedere aut judicare* principle); and, to that end, that each State will exercise the jurisdictions given to it. The early Conventions limited jurisdiction territorially. Thus, the Hague Convention on the Hijacking of Aircraft of 1970 allowed a State jurisdiction over a crime committed in its territory, its registered aircraft and when the plane lands on its territory with the offender on board. Later Conventions appreciably extended jurisdiction. Thus, the Terrorist Bombings Convention of 1997 conferred jurisdiction over a crime committed in its territory or on its ships and aircraft (territoriality), or committed anywhere by its nationals (nationality); and allowed a State to establish further jurisdictional competence where the offence is committed against a national (passive personality) or against a Government facility abroad (security).

Lockerbie

Jurisdictional issues arose out of the downing of Pan Am Flight 103 over Lockerbie in December 1988, in which all 259 passengers and crew were killed along with 11 residents of the town – the largest terrorist atrocity at the time, and only eclipsed in scale by 9/11. As the explosion occurred and the bodies and debris were recovered in Scotland, Scotland had jurisdiction under the territorial principle; the US also had jurisdiction as the Pan Am 747 was American registered. In November 1991, indictments in virtually identical terms were handed down in Scotland and in Washington DC against two Libyans. As Libya had no extradition treaties with the UK or US, Libya declined to extradite the accused, insisting that it use the option available in the Montreal Convention on Aircraft Sabotage of 1971 to prosecute the accused itself. This being unacceptable to the UK and US, they sought, and obtained, a demand from the Security Council for the surrender of the accused backed by sanctions. In 1998, a compromise was reached, endorsed by the Security Council, that the Libyans be surrendered for trial in a neutral venue (Camp Zeist in the Netherlands) by a court of three judges (and no jury), but otherwise conducted as a normal Scottish trial under solemn procedure. In 2001, one of the two accused was convicted (*HM Advocate* v *Megrahi* (2000)); his appeal was unsuccessful (*Megrahi* v *HM Advocate* (2002)).

IMMUNITIES FROM JURISDICTION

The territoriality of jurisdiction admits of some exceptions, principally in relation to foreign States and their representatives. At one time, a foreign State, its ruler, its official representatives and its property were not regarded as amenable to the jurisdiction of any State's courts. This principle was stated by the Court of Appeal in *Parlement Belge* (1880) in these terms:

> "... as a consequence of the absolute independence of every sovereign authority, and of the international comity which induces every sovereign State to respect the independence and dignity of every other sovereign State, each and every one declines to exercise by means of its courts any of its territorial jurisdiction over the person of any sovereign or ambassador of any other State, or over the public property of any State which is destined to public use, or over the property of any ambassador, though such sovereign, ambassador or property be within its territory, and therefore, but for the common agreement, subject to its jurisdiction."

In more modern times, a distinction has been drawn between the immunity accorded to a State itself, its ruler and its property (called State or sovereign immunity) and immunity accorded to a State's official representatives (called diplomatic and consular immunity); and within the last century, the absolute nature of these State and diplomatic and consular immunities has been considerably curtailed and the law on diplomatic and consular immunities has been codified and clarified.

State immunity

The traditional rule was to the effect that, all States being equal, no State could subject another State to its jurisdiction. This applied particularly to a Head of State. So, the Court of Appeal granted immunity to the Sultan of

Johore in an action for breach of promise to marry brought by an English woman, even though the Sultan was in England incognito, passing himself off as "Albert Baker", the court declaring a Head of State's immunity to be "laid down absolutely and without any qualification" (*Mighell* v *Sultan of Johore* (1894)).

The immunity of a serving Head of State (or Government) from criminal proceedings extends to serving members of a State's Government. In the *Arrest Warrant Case* (2002), the ICJ held that a Belgian arrest warrant against the Democratic Republic of Congo's Minister for Foreign Affairs on charges of breaching international humanitarian law violated the immunity enjoyed by the Minister under international law. It seems that, following the House of Lords' final decision in the extradition application by Spain in respect of former Chilean President Augusto Pinochet (*ex parte Pinochet (No 3)* (2000)), a former Head of State would have no immunity unless the acts were committed in an official, and not a private, capacity; and no immunity for acts committed in violation of a Convention, like the Torture Convention, to which the State of which the individual was head was a party, it being accepted that no Head of State can act contrary to the fundamental tenets of international humanitarian law and claim the acts were performed in an official capacity. The same rules are thought to extend beyond heads of State to former Ministers in a Government.

The absolute civil immunity of State property, exemplified in cases like *Parlement Belge, Porto Alexandra* (1920) and *Cristina* (1938), began to give place to a more restrictive doctrine. As expressed in the so-called Tate letter of 1952, as a matter of US policy, immunity would continue "with respect to sovereign or public acts (*jure imperii*) of a state, but not with respect to private acts (*jure gestionis*)". This distinction between public and private acts (or sovereign and commercial acts) was necessitated by the realities of trading with Communist countries, where all property was held, and all contracts concluded, by agencies of the State. Restricting civil immunity to sovereign or public acts made sound commercial sense for many States and the practice developed of denying State immunity in respect of commercial acts: see *Philippine Admiral* (1977); *Trendex Trading Corp* v *Central Bank of Nigeria* (1977); *I Congresso del Partido* (1983).

The restrictive doctrine of State immunity is now enshrined in the State Immunity Act 1978 and in similar legislation in many other countries. In addition, the European Convention on State Immunity of 1972 and the International Law Commission's Draft Articles on the Jurisdictional Immunities of States and their Property of 1991 restate the same principle, establishing beyond doubt that the restrictive doctrine is now part of customary law.

Diplomatic and consular immunities and privileges

Certain accepted protections for ambassadors and other representatives of States have been part of international law from its earliest days. These protections, in the form of some immunities from local jurisdiction and privileges in the host State, evolved over the years in customary law; and they were always regarded as of fundamental importance to the international community. In the *Tehran Hostages Case* (1980), when 52 US citizens, 50 with diplomatic status, were held in the American embassy in Tehran for 444 days by pro-revolutionary students and demonstrators, in a rare unanimous judgment, the ICJ said:

> "Such events cannot fail to undermine the edifice of law carefully constructed by mankind over a period of centuries, the maintenance of which is vital for the security and well-being of the complex international community of the present day, to which it is more essential than ever that the rules developed to ensure the ordered progress of relations between its members should be constantly and scrupulously respected."

Following extensive study by the International Law Commission, the rules of diplomatic and consular law were codified (and, to a limited extent, progressively developed) in two Conventions, the Vienna Convention on Diplomatic Relations of 1961 and the Vienna Convention of Consular Relations of 1963. The law, as enshrined in these Conventions, is widely accepted (with 186 and 172 parties respectively) and respected, and there are few areas of controversy.

Under the Vienna Convention on Diplomatic Relations, a diplomatic agent (defined as the head of the mission or a member of the diplomatic staff, and family members forming part of their household) enjoys complete immunity from criminal, civil and administrative jurisdiction, except in relation to actions involving private immovable property, succession and private professional or commercial activity. Lesser personnel in a mission do not enjoy the same extent of immunity: administrative and technical staff (and their families) enjoy complete immunity from criminal jurisdiction, but their immunity from civil and administrative jurisdiction does not extend to acts performed outside the course of their duties; and service staff enjoy immunity from criminal, civil and administrative jurisdiction only in respect of acts performed in the course of their duties. Immunity may be waived by the sending State.

The premises of a mission and the archives and documents of the mission are all inviolable. Freedom of communication, including the use of a diplomatic courier and diplomatic bag, is guaranteed. Nonetheless, all persons enjoying privileges and immunities are obliged to respect the laws and regulations of the receiving State, and the mission is not to be used in a manner incompatible with its functions.

The Vienna Convention on Consular Relations seeks to assimilate the privileges and immunities of consuls with those of diplomats. Consular officers are granted immunity from the jurisdiction of judicial and administrative authorities in respect of acts performed in the exercise of consular functions, and consular premises, archives and documents are inviolable.

The ICJ has had occasion to rule three times on the meaning of Art 36 of the Vienna Convention on Consular Relations, in the *Breard* (1998), *LaGrand* (1999) and *Avenna* (2004) cases, and three times it has ruled that the US failed to notify foreign nationals (of Bolivia, Germany and Mexico respectively) of their right on arrest on criminal charges to have access to consular assistance. While the requirement of notification of the right to consular access is clear, the Court's insistence, in *LaGrand* and *Avenna*, that there must be a review of the convictions secured after a breach of Art 36 has caused problems for the US, whose municipal law has provisions precluding review of convictions on issues not raised at trial or on appeal (called the procedural default rule).

Essential Facts

- The sovereignty of a State comprises both its exclusive authority over its territory and the people on it and its legal equality with all other States.

- There are three principal methods by which can acquire title to territory: occupation, prescription (sometimes now called consolidation) and cession.

- The primary basis for a State exercising criminal jurisdiction is territorial. Among the extra-territorial bases are jurisdiction over its own nationals and over foreigners for crimes committed against its security or its nationals or for international crimes of a particularly heinous nature.

- Immune from the jurisdiction of a State are foreign States, their rulers and their property used for public purposes and those with diplomatic or consular status.

Essential Cases

Island of Palmas Case (1928): this arbitration awarded title to the island to the Netherlands, preferring its claim to that of the US because the Netherlands had exercised more and longer governmental authority than the other claimant.

Lotus Case (1927): the World Court held that there was no rule of international law preventing Turkey from exercising jurisdiction over a Frenchman in respect of a high seas collision resulting in the death of eight Turkish nationals.

Tehran Hostages Case (1980): the ICJ held Iran responsible for the storming and seizure of US diplomatic premises by pro-revolutionary groups, describing diplomatic inviolability as "vital" to the international community.

7 STATE RESPONSIBILITY

State responsibility is concerned with the legal consequences of an internationally wrongful act by a State, addressing the obligations of the wrongdoer, on the one hand, and the rights and powers of any State affected by the wrongdoing, on the other.

In 2001, after some 45 years' work on the subject, the International Law Commission adopted Draft Articles on State Responsibility. While the Draft Articles have not been incorporated into an international Convention and are not legally binding, they are generally regarded as being reflective of customary international law: *Gabčikovo Nagymaros Project Case* (1997). The ILC addressed the legal consequences of any internationally wrongful act, and not the substance and content of particular international wrongs. As a result, the substantive content of State responsibility is left by the ILC as nothing more than the definition of an internationally wrongful act, being a "breach of an international obligation of a State" (Art 2). It does not matter whether the breached international obligation derives from custom, treaty or some other source; nor does it matter that the wrongful act is not characterised as such in municipal law.

The basic principle of State responsibility, articulated in Art 1 of the Draft Articles, is that "Every internationally wrongful act of a State entails the international responsibility of that State". The broad consequence of international responsibility was expressed by the PCIJ in the *Chorzow Factory (Indemnity) Case* (1928) in these terms: "any breach of an international engagement involves an obligation to make reparation" – in the sense of making good the damage caused by the wrong, and not necessarily simply paying monetary compensation.

INTERNATIONAL WRONGS

Preceding issues concerning the consequences of international wrongs is the question of what specific acts or omissions of a State give rise to legal liability. While no distinction is made between contractual and non-contractual liability, a distinction was for a time made between international crimes and international delicts. Earlier versions of the Draft Articles considered certain obligations to be so essential for the protection of the fundamental interests of the international community that breaches should be recognised as crimes. However, many considered the distinction to be unjustifiable, not least because of the difficulty of imposing penal sanction on States, and it was abandoned before the 2001 Draft Articles.

The breach of a treaty (as was the subject-matter of the *Gabčikovo Nagymaros Project Case* (1997)), an attack by the military forces of one State against another (as in the Iraqi invasion of Kuwait in August 1990) and a failure of a State to protect a foreign embassy and its personnel from violence by demonstrators (as was the subject-matter of the *Tehran Hostages Case* (1980)) are but three examples of international wrongs committed directly by one State on another. But State responsibility is more correctly thought of in terms of wrongs committed by a State not against another State, but against foreign nationals or foreign companies. Two such particular wrongs have, over the years, given rise to some legal controversy.

Expropriation

The notion of expropriation, ie the compulsory divestment of ownership of property for public purposes, is familiar in municipal law, but neither the concept nor the terminology associated with it is precise. Expropriation is of significance in international law when it is carried out by a State in relation to the property of nationals, or more likely companies, of another State.

It has long been accepted that, as an aspect or incident of its sovereignty, a State has the right to expropriate anything within its territory, a right recognised in the Declaration on Permanent Sovereignty over Natural Resources of 1962. Paragraph 4 of that resolution set conditions on expropriation, conditions accepted in the *Texaco–Libya Arbitration* (1977), as representing customary law: it must be based:

> "on grounds or reasons of public utility, security or the national interest which are recognized as overriding purely individual or private interests, both domestic and foreign. In such cases the owner shall be paid appropriate compensation ..."

In practice, the requirements that there be a public purpose in the taking and that there be no discrimination against foreigners tend to be discounted as attention is focused on the payment of "appropriate compensation". The major capital exporting States take the view that compensation is appropriate when it is promptly paid (or promptly determined with interest on deferred payment), adequate as to amount (the market value to the owner) and effective (usable by the owner). Developing States take a radically different view, founding on the so-called New International Economic Order as set out in a number of General Assembly resolutions, particularly the Charter of Economic Rights and Duties of States of 1974 . Under these resolutions, compensation for expropriation is not mandatory, and the expropriating State is free to compensate or not and in any amount determined by its own law. The *Texaco–Libya Arbitration* favoured the Resolution 1803 standards.

In many cases, expropriation is effected through the cancellation by a State of a concession contract it has with a foreign company. Such a contract is usually stated to be governed by the law of the contracting State, and not by international law; and it usually contains provision for the settlement of disputes by international arbitration. Such a State contract is obviously not a treaty, being merely a contract under the law of the contracting State, but may become "internationalised" or "de-localised" if the State breaches it in a way that only a State can, as by executive decree or legislative act. These breaches elevate the contract to the international plane, with the result that it is possible to apply international law to it.

Denial of justice

This inexact term, clearly covering situations in which a foreign national is denied justice by a court, has been argued to include any failure on the part of organs charged with administering justice to conform to international standards in their treatment of aliens. On the narrow view, refusing foreigners access to courts or a consistent line of decisions against foreigners would be denials of justice; on the broad view, abuse and maltreatment by immigration, customs, police and prison officials would also be denials of justice. There is even a view that the failure of a State to take reasonable steps to protect foreigners in a situation where they are known to be at risk of violence constitutes a denial of justice.

For a claim based on denial of justice to succeed, the State's conduct, of commission or omission, must be perceptibly lamentable. As was said in the *Neer Claim* (1926), the State's shortcomings must amount "to an outrage, to bad faith, to wilful neglect of duty, or to an insufficiency of governmental action so far short of international standards that every reasonable and impartial man would readily recognise its insufficiency". This is referred to as the international minimum standard, a baseline for the behaviour of civilized States.

There is an increasing tendency to adapt the standard to that of national treatment, requiring that foreigners be treated no worse than nationals, though these remains an irreducible minimum standard. In the *Roberts Claim* (1926), Henry Roberts, an American citizen, was held in a Mexican jail, described by an arbitral tribunal in these terms:

"he was kept in a room thirty-five feet long and twenty feet wide with stone walls, earthen floor, straw roof, a single window, a single door and no sanitary accommodations, all the prisoners depositing their excrement in a barrel kept in a corner of the room; thirty or forty men were at times thrown together in this single room; the prisoners were given no facilities to clean themselves; the room contained no furniture except that which the prisoners were able to obtain by their own means; they were afforded no opportunity to take physical exercise; and the food given them was scarce, unclean, and of the coarsest kind".

Mexico's defence that Roberts was accorded exactly the same treatment as Mexican nationals failed, the tribunal ruling that the true test was "whether aliens are treated in accordance with ordinary standards of civilization".

Most denials of justice would now fall within the purview of the Universal Declaration of Human Rights of 1948 and the International Covenant on Civil and Political Rights of 1966, setting standards for the treatment of all people within a State, nationals and aliens (see Chapter 9). The distinction between an international minimum standard and a national treatment standard has no application in human rights law.

INTERNATIONAL CLAIMS

Individuals or companies of one State harmed as a result of an international wrong by another State have no procedural capacity in international law (absent specific treaty authority). They must turn to their national State for representation on the international plane. The fiction of international law is that an international wrong, perpetrated against a State's nationals or national companies, is a wrong committed against it. As was said in the *Mavrommatis Palestine Concessions Case* (1924):

"By taking up the case of one of its subjects and by resorting to diplomatic action or international judicial proceedings on his behalf, a State is in reality asserting its own rights – its right to ensure, in the person of its subjects, respect for the rules of international law."

The wrong being deemed to have been done to the State, it falls to the State, in its discretion, to determine whether it will espouse the claim or not and, if it espouses the claim, how it will pursue and settle the claim.

Attribution

The ILC Draft Articles, in defining the elements of an internationally wrongful act in Art 2, require that the breach of an international obligation "is attributable to the State under international law". Given that a State, an abstract entity, has in itself no capacity to act, the rules on attribution identify the organs and individuals in it that can, by their conduct in breach of international law, attract international responsibility.

Conduct is attributable to a State where it is undertaken by a State organ, "whether the organ exercises legislative, executive, judicial or any other functions, whatever position it holds in the organisation of the State, and whatever its character as an organ of the central government or as of a territorial unit of the State" (Art 4). The conduct of persons or entities exercising elements of governmental authority are attributable to the State (Art 5). The State will not escape responsibility "even where the organ or individual exceeds its authority or contravenes instructions" (Art 7).

There is a presumption that a State is not responsible for the acts of private individuals: However, conduct of an individual or group of individuals which is directed or controlled by a State (Art 8), and conduct by an individual or group of individuals which factually amounts to the exercise of governmental authority and which is carried out in the absence or default of the official authorities of a State (Art 9), are attributable to the State. Many of the problems on attribution have related to insurrections or uprisings within States. Where an uprising is successful in establishing a new Government, its conduct in breach of international law during the insurrection will be attributable to the State (Art 10). However, the conduct of unsuccessful uprisings is not attributable to the State.

Nationality of claims

The right of a State to invoke international wrongs against another State "is necessarily limited to intervention on behalf of its own nationals because, in the absence of a special agreement, it is the bond of nationality between the State and the individual which alone confers upon the State the right of diplomatic protection, and it is as a part of the function of diplomatic protection that the right to take up a claim and to ensure respect for the rules of international law must be envisaged": *Panevezys-Saldutiskis Railway Case* (1939).

The ILC Draft Articles on State Responsibility contain only the briefest reference to the nationality of claims rule, the rule itself being the subject of the ILC's Draft Articles on Diplomatic Protection of 2006.

Generally, international law leaves it to each State to determine who has its nationality: *Nationality Decrees of Tunis and Morocco Case* (1923). Where nationality is invoked as the basis for the exercise of diplomatic protection, it must satisfy certain requirements laid down by international law: *Nottebohm Case* (1955); Draft Articles on Diplomatic Protection,

Arts 4 and 9. In the case of both natural and legal persons, the claimant must be a national not only at the time of the claim's presentation, but also continuously during the whole time since the injury occurred: *Panevezys-Saldutiskis Railway Case* (1939); Draft Articles on Diplomatic Protection, Arts 5 and 10.

While a State is free to confer its nationality on an individual subject to any conditions it chooses, and that grant of nationality is effective for internal, municipal purposes (such as the right to vote, receipt of social benefits), it is effective for the right of diplomatic protection only if there is a genuine link between the individual and the State. In the *Nottebohm Case* (1955), Liechtenstein was not entitled to pursue a claim on behalf of a naturalised citizen, Frederic Nottebohm, because he had virtually no links whatever with Liechtenstein. The ICJ's decision established the "genuine link" test, but the actual application of the test was unfortunate for Nottebohm in that, having renounced his original German nationality, not having sought or been granted Guatemalan citizenship (where he lived and worked) and having only Liechtenstein nationality by naturalisation, he was effectively rendered stateless.

Individuals with dual, or even multiple, nationalities have in the past caused some difficulties in identifying which national State is entitled to exercise diplomatic protection. In relation to any State of which the individual is not a national, any national State may exercise diplomatic protection or they may do so jointly: Draft Articles on Diplomatic Protection, Art 6. However, in relation to a State of which the individual is a national, it is only the national State with "predominant" nationality that can act: Art 7. The earlier case law, notably the *Mergé Claim* (1955), talked in terms of the effective – meaning more or most effective – nationality. The terms "predominant" and "effective" have the same import, that it is the State with the greater or greatest links that can pursue a claim.

In fact, it was this test for dual and multiple nationalities that the ICJ used in the *Nottebohm Case*, even though Nottebohm at the time had only one nationality. It was Nottebohm's strong links with Guatemala and lack of any credible links with Liechtenstein that led the Court to conclude that Liechtenstein could not pursue an international claim on Nottebohm's behalf against Guatemala.

For the purposes of diplomatic protection, a company has the nationality of the State under whose laws it is incorporated. This was determined in the *Barcelona Traction Co Case (Second Phase)* (1970), in which the ICJ held that the Barcelona Traction Company, incorporated in Canada, had Canadian nationality, despite not trading in Canada and having some 88 per cent of its shares held by Belgian nationals. It rejected other possible bases of nationality, including the *siège social* (centre of management or control) and the beneficial interests test (the State of nationality of the bulk of the shareholders), and reiterated the State of incorporation as the test. This test has been slightly adapted in Art 9 of the Draft Articles on Diplomatic Protection, providing that, while the State of incorporation is the primary test, when a company is controlled from abroad and conducts its business abroad, the seat of management and financial control is to determine its nationality.

Exhaustion of local remedies

This "important principle of customary international law" (*ELSI Case* (1989)) has been explained by the ICJ in the *Interhandel Case* (1959) in these terms;

> "The rule that local remedies must be exhausted before international proceedings may be instituted is a well-established rule of customary international law; the rule has been generally observed in cases in which a State has adopted the cause of its national whose rights are claimed to have been disregarded in another State in violation of international law. Before resort may be had to an international court in such a situation, it has been considered necessary that the State where the violation occurred should have an opportunity to redress it by its own means, within the framework of its own domestic legal system."

The requirement is for the exhaustion of "any available and effective local remedy": Draft Articles on State Responsibility, Art 44. Local remedies include all effective remedies available to natural or legal persons under the domestic law of the State concerned and capable of redressing the situation complained of, whether judicial or administrative, ordinary or extraordinary, of the first, second or third instance, including procedural means and other formal remedies. In general, the injured individual or company must advance all legal grounds and arguments calculated to achieve a favourable decision. In the *Ambatielos Arbitration* (1956), when a Greek national did not call an essential witness at trial or in the Court of Appeal and did not pursue his appeal against the Board of Trade to the House of Lords, an arbitral tribunal held that he had not exhausted all remedies available to him.

However, the requirement falls where there are no effective remedies. "There can be no need to resort to the municipal courts if those courts have no jurisdiction to afford relief; nor is it necessary again to resort to those courts if the result must be a repetition of a decision already given": *Panevezys-Saldutiskis Railway Case* (1939). The ILC Draft Articles on

Diplomatic Protection, in Art 15, list circumstances in which there is no need to exhaust local remedies, including where there are no reasonably available local remedies to provide effective redress, there is undue delay in the remedial process or the injured person is manifestly precluded from pursuing local remedies.

International remedies

Article 34 of the Draft Articles on State Responsibility provides that reparation for an international wrong "shall take the form of restitution, compensation and satisfaction, either singly or in combination". Restitution involves re-establishing as far as possible the situation which existed before the wrongful act was committed. As was said in the *Chorzow Factory Case* (1928), the primary form of reparation is "the obligation to restore the undertaking and, if this be not possible, to pay its value at the time of the indemnification, which value is designed to take the place of restitution which has become impossible".

Article 36 provides that the States responsible for an international wrong "is under an obligation to compensate for the damage caused thereby, insofar as such damage is not made good by restitution" and that "compensation shall cover any financially assessable damage including loss of profits". The aim of compensation is, in the words of the tribunal in the *Lusitania Case* (1923), that "the remedy should be commensurate with the loss, so that the injured party may be made whole". In determining the heads of compensable damage and the amount of compensation, there are no hard and fast rules; these will vary, depending upon the content of the breached international obligations, the behaviour of the parties and, more generally, a concern to reach an equitable and acceptable outcome.

The third form of reparation − satisfaction − "may consist in an acknowledgement of the breach, an expression of regret, a formal apology or another appropriate modality"; but it must not "be out of proportion to the injury and may not take a form humiliating to the responsible State": Art 37.

The Draft Articles on State Responsibility also address self-help measures by States, referring to them as counter-measures, a term introduced into the language of international law by the *Air Transport Services Arbitration* (1978). If a State seeks to remedy a international wrong by itself, it will be acting lawfully if it complies with the requirements set out in the Draft Articles, even if its actions would be otherwise unlawful. Lawful countermeasures must only be taken to induce compliance with the earlier wrong (Art 49); they must be proportionate (Art 51); and they must be terminated when the responsible State has complied with its obligation (Art 53). Lawful countermeasures cannot involve the threat or use of force (Art 50).

Essential Facts

- A State is responsible under international law for internationally wrongful acts and must make good any harm or damage caused by these acts.
- A State is responsible for the acts of its organs, its officers and its officials and, in limited circumstances, for the acts of individual citizens.
- Before a State can pursue an international claim on behalf of one of its citizens or companies, it must ensure that the aggrieved individual or company has its nationality and has exhausted all local remedies in the wrong-doing State.

Essential Cases

Nottebohm Case (1955): the ICJ held that a naturalised Liechtenstein citizen, who had lived and worked most of his life in Guatemala, did not have a genuine link with Liechtenstein sufficient to permit Liechtenstein to pursue an international claim on his behalf against Guatemala.

Barcelona Traction Co Case (1970): in examining which State was entitled to bring an international claim on a behalf of a company incorporated in Canada, but trading in Spain, and with the vast bulk of its shares held by Belgian nationals, the ICJ held that the company had the nationality of the State in which it was incorporated.

Ambatielos Arbitration (1956): when a Greek national with a grievance against the UK Board of Trade did not call a witness at trial and on his first appeal and then failed to make his second available appeal, an arbitral tribunal held that he had not exhausted local remedies.

8 USE OF FORCE

The international legal rules on the use of force determine the circumstances in which a State's resort to armed force is permissible or impermissible. This is the *jus ad bellum*, the right to resort to war, to be contrasted with the *jus in bello*, the laws of war, now more frequently called international humanitarian law (see Chapter 9). The laws on the conduct of hostilities developed from about the middle of the 19th century, but it was a century later before the *jus ad bellum* became radically changed from its traditional rules.

TRADITIONAL RULES

Traditionally, there was little regulation on a State's use of force. Indeed, the use of force against another State was regarded as one of the weapons in its foreign policy arsenal. An aspect of its sovereignty, the use of force was one means by which a State could redress a grievance or pursue a territorial or other claim. Up till 1945, any territorial acquisition by the use of force, referred to as conquest and subjugation (see Chapter 6), was legitimate. The Roman empire was acquired by conquest, as were many of the later empires that dominated the world. Even parts of the British empire were acquired by a process, if not of conquest, then of something very similar.

The only limitations on this absolute right to use force were of a moral or religious nature. Normally associated with Thomas Aquinas, the just war doctrine postulated that war must have a just cause and be waged by just means. A just cause would be redress of a serious grievance that has gone unanswered or self-defence against an attack; an unjust cause would be an unprovoked attack or the use of force for material gain. The just war doctrine was developed from the 13th century, mainly by Catholic theologians and scholars, but it never attained the status of law. Throughout its currency, it was a moral and political basis for State action; it was a justification used by States when resorting to war.

The ascendency of positive legal thought in the 19th century, with its emphasis on State sovereignty and a limited role for international law, eliminated many moral considerations from the law. The carnage of World War I (with some 37 million deaths) shocked States into action, that action being the creation of the League of Nations in 1919, which was intended to prevent a recurrence of the events that happened in Europe between 1914 and 1918. The fact that there was a recurrence of these events within 20 years proved that the Covenant of the League was defective in addressing the maintenance of peace and security and, equally, that States were not ready to accept limitations on their freedom to use force. Nonetheless, in 1928, 15 major powers agreed in the Kellogg–Briand Pact that they would not use war an instrument on national policy and would settle all controversies by peaceful means. This promising sign was negated by the subsequent invasion of Manchuria by Japan in 1931, Ethiopia by Italy in 1935 and the Rhineland (and later much of Western Europe) by Germany in 1936.

Some 50–70 million deaths in World War II convinced the international community that something had to be done about the easy recourse to war and, to that end, a new international organisation, the United Nations, was created to replace the League of Nations with a body with real powers to ensure international peace and security.

ARTICLE 2(4)

The first prohibition in international law on the use of force by States is contained in Art 2(4) of the UN Charter:

> "All Members shall refrain in their international relations from the threat or use of force against the territorial integrity or political independence of any state, or in any other manner inconsistent with the Purposes of the United Nations."

The drafters of the Charter intended Art 2(4) to be read with Art 2(3), requiring that all disputes are to be settled by peaceful means. While Art 2(4) was new to international law, there was a long-standing obligation on States to settle disputes peacefully: a Hague Convention for the Pacific Settlement of Disputes of 1899 articulated the obligation, which was repeated in many subsequent instruments.

There is no doubt but that the prohibition contained in Art 2(4) is not only customary international law, but also *jus cogens*: *Military and Paramilitary Activities Case (Merits)* (1986). Thus, from a position prior to 1945 when the use of force was permissible except when specifically prohibited by treaty, international law has moved to the complete outlawry of force (save for two exceptions), applicable to all States, whether parties to the UN Charter or not, and of a status higher than any regular custom or treaty.

The extent of this prohibition is discernible from the Friendly Relations Declaration of 1970, a General Assembly resolution intended as an authoritative interpretation of the Charter. Illegal force is constituted by, for example, wars of aggression (as in the Iraqi invasion of Kuwait in 1990); organising or encouraging irregular forces within another State and participating in civil strife in another State (both as in the US activities in Nicaragua in support of the Contra rebels in the early 1980s, the subject of the *Military and Paramilitary Activities Case*); and wars in violation of boundaries (again as in the Iraqi invasion of Kuwait).

This prohibition admits of two clear exceptions. The first relates to the right of self-defence, as expressed in Art 51 of the Charter; and the second to action taken, or authorised, by the UN Security Council, as expressed in Chapter VII of the Charter, particularly Art 42.

SELF-DEFENCE

Customary law

Self-defence has long been accepted as a justification for the use of force in international law; it was, for instance, so regarded by adherents to the just war doctrine. However, its exact parameters were unclear until the mid-19th century, when a test was articulated in correspondence between the UK and US Governments over the *Caroline Incident* in 1837. The *Caroline* test has two components: urgent necessity and proportionality. In the words of the correspondence, the necessity for exercising self-defence must be "instant, overwhelming, leaving no choice of means or moment for deliberation"; and the response must involve "nothing unreasonable or excessive, since the act justified by the necessity of self-defence must be limited by that necessity and kept clearly within it".

Article 51

Self-defence, as defined in *Caroline*, was part of customary international law before Art 51 of the UN Charter, which sets out a slightly different articulation of self-defence:

> "Nothing in the present Charter shall impair the inherent right of individual or collective self-defence if an armed attack occurs against a Member of the United Nations, until the Security Council has taken measures necessary to maintain international peace and security."

The Art 51 test assumes that there is an existing ("inherent") right to self-defence, which can only mean the right articulated in *Caroline*. It also requires an "armed attack", something not explicitly required by the customary test, though the facts of the *Caroline* incident, in which British troops attacked and sank an American vessel assisting rebels in Canada, involved an armed attack. The customary test clearly views self-defence as an individual right in one State to react to violence by another State. Recognising that a weak State would have little prospect of successfully defending itself against a stronger aggressor, Art 51 allows for collective self-defence, whereby a weak State (or indeed any State) can seek the assistance of other States in defending itself. It is also noticeable that Art 51 envisages self-defence as temporary, being urgent action taken by a State until such time as the UN Security Council can exercise its powers under Chapter VII of the Charter.

The question arises as to whether, post 1945, there is one test for self-defence (the Art 51 test) or two (the Art 51 and *Caroline* tests). It might appear that Art 51, being contained in the UN Charter, would override the older customary test, but, in fact, it seems that both have continued. The difficulty here is that issues of self-defence occur in political fora, frequently the Security Council, where States perceiving themselves at risk tend to argue in political, rather than legal, terms. As a result, it is often unclear whether a State claiming the right to self-defence is claiming that right as part of customary or conventional law or – indeed some combination of the two.

Anticipatory self-defence

Article 51 specifically requiring an "armed attack", self-defence cannot be anticipatory in the sense of permitting the reactive use of force before an armed attack. In relation to self-defence under the *Caroline* test, which does not explicitly require an armed attack, the determining factor would be urgent necessity. A hostile neighbour amassing troops on a border, apparently poised to attack a State, would, it can be argued, permit the exercise by that State of self-defence under the customary test.

In an era of nuclear weapons and other weapons of mass destruction, it would be suicide for a State to await an actual attack before responding. The prohibition in Art 2(4) of the "threat" as well as the "use" of force has raised the possibility of allowing self-defence if the threat of attack is imminent enough and the potential consequences serious enough. This proposition was given limited support by the International Court in the *Legality of the Threat or Use of Nuclear Weapons Case* (1996), in which the

Court held back from condemning a pre-emptive nuclear response when the very survival of a State was in jeopardy.

Nonetheless, most States and most commentators on international law do not accept a right of anticipatory self-defence, mainly because of the risk of abuse. Anticipatory self-defence could, if permissible, be used by any State feeling at any risk from a neighbour, thereby undermining the cardinal prohibition on any use of force.

Bush doctrine

In the aftermath of 9/11, and concerned about "rogue" States, terrorists and the use of weapons of mass destruction as "weapons of choice", President George W Bush redefined the circumstances justifying the exercise of the right of (anticipatory) self-defence. He asserted that international law recognised that a State could defend itself against "an imminent danger of attack", and need not wait for an actual attack; in such circumstances, the US claimed the right to act "pre-emptively."

The Bush doctrine has received little support from other States. It runs counter to the long-held US position that required an armed attack to trigger the right to self-defence. If anticipatory self-defence, involving an imminent attack, is dubious, so much more must be the Bush doctrine, involving as it does an imminent threat of attack.

SECURITY COUNCIL ACTION

Given the failures of the League of Nations' arrangements for maintaining international peace and security, the drafters of the UN Charter were determined to give a central and controlling role to the Security Council. A scheme for ensuring international peace and security is set out in Chapter VII of the Charter, the operation of which is intended to be staged.

First, when any threatening dispute is brought to the attention of the Security Council, it has the power to decide whether the situation is a threat to the peace, breach of the peace or act of aggression (Art 39). It does not matter which of these three is determined to exist. When Iraq invaded Kuwait in August 1990, a clear act of aggression, the Security Council in Resolution 660 (1990) characterised the situation as a breach of the peace.

The determination that there is a threat to or breach of the peace or an aggression triggers for the Security Council the full powers set out in Chapter VII, referred to as enforcement action. It may impose sanctions under Art 41 and these "may include complete or partial interruption of economic relations and of rail, sea, air, postal, telegraphic, radio, and other means of communication, and the severance of diplomatic relations". These sanctions are mandatory and must be implemented and enforced by all UN members. At present, the Security Council has sanctions under Art 41 imposed on 12 States or other entities, including Liberia, Somalia, Sudan and the Taliban.

If the Security Council considers that sanctions have not worked or, if imposed, would not work, it may use force. In the words of Art 42, "it may take such action by air, sea, or land forces as may be necessary to maintain or restore international peace and security". To that end, the Security Council may demand the assistance of all or some of the member States (Art 48) or of regional organisations, such a NATO (Art 53).

The original plan was for the Security Council to take military action itself when necessary. It was to have forces and *materiel* contributed by Member States through agreements with the UN (Art 43) and a command structure through the Military Staff Committee of the chiefs-of-staff of the permanent members (Arts 46–47). However, no agreements were concluded between the UN and States for the provision of personnel and *materiel*; and, as a consequence the Military Staff Committee was moribund.

The Security Council has therefore never utilised its power in Art 42 to use force. Instead, it has devised another process, whereby, rather than acting itself, it authorises States to act to achieve set goals. In so doing, States are not acting as organs or agents of the Security Council or the UN; they are acting on the Security Council's authorisation, as provided for in Art 48 of the Charter – and, if not specifically in that article, from the penumbra of powers conferred on the Security Council in Chapter VII of the Charter.

The Security Council authorisation is invariably expressed in general terms. So, in landmark Resolution 678 (1990), designed to remove Iraq from Kuwait, the Security Council:

"Authorizes Member States co-operating with the Government of Kuwait, unless Iraq on or before 15 January 1991 fully implements ... the above-mentioned resolutions, to use all necessary means to uphold and implement resolution 660 (1990) and all subsequent relevant resolutions and to restore international peace and security in the area."

The term "use all necessary means" is code for the use of force. The conferred authority is broadly expressed: to ensure compliance with its earlier demands for the withdrawal of Iraq from Kuwait and the restoration of stability in the region. Apart from setting the goals and the earliest starting date of hostilities (they began on 17 January 1991), the Security Council played no role in the conduct of hostilities; it did not even determine when the hostilities should cease (they ceased on 28 February 1991), that being a decision taken by the 34-State coalition led by the US.

HUMANITARIAN INTERVENTION

It remains a vexed question in international law whether a State, or group of States, can intervene militarily to protect the citizens of another State from egregious human rights abuses by their own Government. Humanitarian intervention in that sense is completely at odds with the prohibition on the use of force in Art 2(4). It also violates one of the cardinal principles of the Friendly Relations Declaration of 1970 that "No State or group of States has the right to intervene, directly or indirectly, for any reason whatever, in the internal or external affairs of any other State".

Nonetheless, humanitarian intervention remains the only possible justification for the NATO bombings of Serbia and Serbian targets in Kosovo in 1999. An Independent International Kosovo Commission subsequently concluded that the NATO action was "illegal but legitimate", implying that, while the use of force satisfied neither of the recognised exceptions to the prohibition on all force, it was morally legitimate in view of the humanitarian catastrophe occurring in Kosovo.

A number of studies by States have likewise concluded that there is no international legal basis for humanitarian intervention. Recognising the atrocities sometimes perpetrated by Governments against their own population, many of these studies, including the Kosovo Commission, have called for the Security Council or General Assembly to formulate rules delineating the circumstances in which States may intervene in other States on humanitarian grounds.

The international response to these calls has been the somewhat feeble "responsibility to protect", articulated in the World Summit Outcome Document of 2005. This responsibility is engaged when a population is experiencing genocide, war crimes, ethnic cleansing or crimes against humanity; and involves nothing more than a vague commitment by the international community to "take collective action, in a timely and decisive manner, through the Security Council, in accordance with the Charter, including Chapter VII, on a case-by-case basis". This is not humanitarian intervention, but a substitute for it, leading to the inevitable conclusion that humanitarian intervention in its traditional sense is unlawful in international law.

APPLICATION OF THE RULES

It is instructive to analyse a few recent and problematic uses of force to see what justifications have been offered. The starting point must be that any use of force is *prima facie* unlawful and that it falls to a State using force to justify that use under one of the two recognised exceptions.

The Gulf war, 1990–91

On 2 August 1990, Iraqi forces invaded Kuwait and occupied the entire territory of the tiny emirate; subsequently Iraq "annexed" Kuwait as its 19th province. Iraq justified its action as an appropriate response to unresolved grievances it had against Kuwait. These grievances included allegations that Kuwait engaged in slant drilling in the Ramallah oilfield straddling the Iraq/Kuwait border, thereby "stealing" Iraqi oil; extracted and sold oil in excess of OPEC quotas; and established military posts on the Iraqi side of the long-disputed border between the two States. None of these grievances – all of which could, and in terms of Art 2(3) of the UN Charter should, have been resolved peacefully – justified the use of force by Iraq.

The Security Council acted immediately in Resolution 660 (1990), adopted on the very day of the invasion, condemning the invasion, calling on Iraq to withdraw and on the two States to settle their differences by negotiation. This resolution, purporting to be adopted under Arts 39 and 40 of the Charter, described the situation as a "breach of international peace and security". On 6 August 1990, the Security Council, expressly acting under Chapter VII of the Charter, imposed comprehensive sanctions against Iraq in Resolution 661 (1990), and that sanctions regime was later refined so as to ameliorate its harmful effect on States seeking to comply and to ensure the supply of humanitarian food and medicine to Iraq.

To remove any doubts about the legality of the interception of vessels thought to be evading the sanctions regime to inspect their cargo, the Security Council in Resolution 665 (1990), again acting under Chapter VII, authorised States "to use such measures commensurate to the specific circumstances as may be necessary" to enforce the sanctions imposed by Resolution 661. Resolution 670 (1990) confirmed that this authorisation extended to aircraft.

When it became clear that political pressure and sanctions were not going to succeed, the Security Council began to consider, as the Charter scheme envisages, the use of force. In its landmark resolution of 29 November 1990, Resolution 678 (1990), the Council authorised the use of force. But was this resolution necessary? In Resolution 661, the Security

Council had already affirmed Kuwait's "inherent right of individual or collective self-defence ... in accordance with Article 51 of the Charter". Kuwait had been subject to an armed attack by Iraq and was, therefore, entitled to invoke the right of self-defence, inviting other States to assist it in exercising that right. Operation Desert Storm, therefore, finds a complete legal justification in self-defence.

Why then adopt a resolution merely adding legality to what was already legal? The explanation, and a particular concern for the UK, is that the lapse of time between the invasion and the earliest possible military response, about 5 months, was at the outer limit the urgency requirement for self-defence. Even allowing for the exigencies of the situation (getting the necessary personnel and *materiel* in place), how could military action in January 1991 be a legitimate response to a situation arising in early August 1990 – be, in *Caroline* terms, "instant, overwhelming, leaving no choice of means or moment for deliberation?". It was thought that it was safest to secure Security Council authorisation for military action against Iraq. Would that such prudence had been employed in 2003 when it was decided to invade Iraq.

Resolution 678, expressly adopted under Chapter VII, authorised those States co-operating with Kuwait (in exercising its right of collective self-defence) "to use all necessary means" to enforce the Council's relevant earlier resolutions (essentially to prise Iraq out of Kuwait) and "to restore international peace and security in the area". As a "pause of goodwill", Iraq was given until 15 January 1991 to comply with the Security Council's resolutions; in truth, the 7-week pause was equally to allow the coalition to amass sufficient personnel and *materiel* to mount an attack on Iraq. Hostilities began on 17 January and the promised "mother of all battles" lasted a mere 42 days, ending with the capitulation of Iraq.

There is no doubt about the legality of this Gulf war. Indeed, it is doubly legal, being justified as collective self-defence under Art 51 of the UN Charter and through explicit authorisation from the Security Council under Chapter VII of the Charter.

Kosovo, 1999

After the fall of Communism in Eastern Europe, the territory of the former Soviet Federal Republic of Yugoslavia fragmented in the Balkan wars. By 1992, Bosnia and Herzegovina, Croatia, Macedonia and Slovenia had broken away, leaving as the Federal Republic of Yugoslavia only Serbia and Montenegro (and it too became independent in 2006). The administration of Slobodan Milosevic, anxious to prevent further territorial losses, tightened its control over the Serbian province of

Kosovo, which, with its mainly ethnic–Albanian Muslim population, had long sought independence from Serbia. Tensions increased when the Kosovo Liberation Army began operations against Yugoslav facilities and personnel in Kosovo, prompting a serious (over)reaction by the Milosevic administration. In the event, Yugoslav police and military activities resulted in the largest population displacement since the 1940s (with an estimated 1 million people ethnically cleansed) and in widespread and systematic atrocities against the people of Kosovo.

Negotiations towards a settlement of the issue having broken down, largely through the intransigence of Milosevic, NATO began air strikes on Serbia and Serbian targets in Kosovo to relieve the plight of the Kosovars on 24 March 1999; the air strikes ended on 10 June 1999 after Yugoslavia's capitulation.

The question arises whether international law permits the use of armed force against Yugoslavia under these circumstances. It is possible to argue that there was an armed attack on Kosovo, but Kosovo, a province of Serbia, was not a State – and the right of self-defence is available only to a State. The Security Council was engaged with the ongoing Kosovan crisis. In Resolution 1199 (1998), the Council expressed deep concern at the deteriorating human rights situation in Kosovo and called on States to provide humanitarian assistance, but it stopped short of authorising the use of force. The resolution was adopted under Chapter VII, its preamble describing the situation as a threat to peace and security in the region, thereby providing the Security Council with the opportunity to invoke sanctions or authorise military force. Because one of the permanent members, Russia, was a long-standing ally of Yugoslavia, the Security Council could not agree then or later to the express authorisation of the use of force.

As a consequence, the NATO military action against Yugoslavia can only be justified as humanitarian intervention and humanitarian intervention is not a recognised exception to the prohibition on the use of force in Art 2(4). The only independent, expert, legal analysis, from the Swedish-sponsored Independent International Kosovo Commission, concluded that the NATO operation in Kosovo was "illegal but legitimate". While morality may have been on NATO's side, international law was not.

Afghanistan, 2001

Afghanistan had attracted the attention of the Security Council before the terrorist atrocities of 11 September 2001 put it firmly in the international spotlight. In Resolution 1214 (1998), the Security Council demanded that Afghanistan cease all discrimination against women and girls, halt the cultivation and trafficking in illegal drugs and "stop providing sanctuary and training for international terrorists and their organisations". That resolution not being adopted under Chapter VII of the Charter and none of its demands being satisfactorily met, a year later, in Resolution 1267 (1999), the Security Council imposed sanctions under Chapter VII, specifically, of course, Art 41. Prophetically, the preamble to the resolution states that the failure of the Taliban authorities to respond to the demand about sanctuary and training for terrorists constituted a threat to international peace and security. The sanctions imposed, involving a flight embargo and the freezing of financial resources, were directed against the Taliban to induce it to meet two specific demands: again, to stop providing sanctuary and training facilities for terrorists; and, additionally, to hand over Osama bin Laden to any State in which he was indicted.

One day after the 9/11 attacks, the Security Council adopted Resolution 1368 (2001), condemning the attacks, expressing condolences to the American people and, significantly, recognising "the inherent right of individual or collective self-defence in accordance with the Charter". The title of the resolution ("Threats to international peace and security caused by terrorist acts") and the context of its adoption mean that the Security Council must have thought that the US had a right of self-defence in respect of the 9/11 attacks.

There is no doubt that the US was the subject of an armed attack, three hijacked aircraft being deliberately flown into the twin towers of the World Trade Center in New York City and the Pentagon just outside Washington DC (a fourth hijacked aircraft crashed into a field in Pennsylvania), with the loss of 2,973 lives. The author of these attacks was the al-Qaeda terrorist group, known to be led by Osama bin Laden, and not any State. Self-defence is posited on an attack on one State by another, not on an attack on a State by a group of individuals. Against whom, then, could the US exercise its Security Council-recognised right of self-defence?

Given that the Taliban, and hence Afghanistan, had, from 1998, been told by the Security Council to stop harbouring and facilitating terrorists in Afghanistan, and that al-Qaeda operated in close collaboration with the Taliban, the governing authority in Afghanistan, it is a small step to attribute the 9/11 attacks to Afghanistan. The American right of self-defence was, thus, exercisable against Afghanistan.

The military response of the US, allied with the UK, on 7 October 2001 was carefully tailored to meet the requirements of self-defence. The US administration announced heightened levels of security alert in the period leading up to and beyond the initial airstrikes against al-Qaeda and Taliban targets so as to emphasise the continuing urgent necessity to act. The terms of engagements for Operation Enduring Freedom were strictly limited to the elimination of terrorist bases in Afghanistan and the seizure of terrorists suspected of involvement in the 9/11 and other atrocities.

The Iraq war, 2003

Following the capitulation of Iraq at the end of the Gulf war, on 3 April 1991, the Security Council adopted Resolution 687 (1991), a resolution imposing extensive obligations on Iraq, including measures to settle the Iraq/Kuwait border, to enable repatriations of individuals and property and to provide compensation for Iraq acts of depredation. Central to this comprehensive resolution was the obligation that Iraq ensure the "destruction, removal and rendering harmless, under international supervision", of all weapons of mass destruction and their delivery systems. To that end, Iraq was required to produce an accounting of all WMDs and their location. International supervision was entrusted to a Special Commission (UNSCOM), charged with inspection and verification functions in Iraq; UNSCOM was to have free access to all Iraqi buildings and facilities. This resolution, which expressly affirmed all 13 previous resolutions on Iraq, including Resolution 678, was adopted under Chapter VII of the Charter. On the acceptance of the resolution by Iraq on 7 April 1991, a "formal ceasefire" was to be effective.

Iraq prevaricated in the production of a complete accounting of its WMDs and continually interfered with United Nations inspections to such an extent that, on 8 November 2002, the Security Council adopted Resolution 1441 (2002), demanding again the full disclosure of all WMDs and "immediate, unimpeded, unconditional, and unrestricted access" to a new monitoring, verification and inspection commission (UNMOVIC), established in 1999 to replace UNSCOM. While UNMOVIC reported to the Security Council that it had been given unrestricted access by the Iraqi authorities, had found no WMDs and had (but could not verify) the full accounting provided by Iraq, the US and UK took the view that Iraq retained WMDs, had hostile intentions towards its neighbours, particularly Israel, had and was supporting international terrorism and had systematically abused its own citizens, particularly the Kurds in the north of the country and Shi'ite "marsh" Arabs in the south.

On 20 March 2003, the American-led "coalition of the willing" began its military invasion of Iraq. Baghdad and the regime of Saddam Hussein fell on 9 April 2003. By 22 May 2003, the Security Council, in Resolution 1483 (2003), recognised the authority – and the responsibilities – of the US and UK "as occupying powers under unified command".

There has been much discussion about the legality of the invasion of Iraq. Certainly, no legal justification can be afforded by the right of self-defence. Nor could legal justification be found in any specific authorisation for the use of force by the Security Council. The legal justification offered derives from the advice (dated 17 March 2003) given to the Cabinet by the British Attorney-General, Lord Goldsmith, in which he asserted that legal authority to use force against Iraq "exists from the combined effect of Resolutions 678, 687 and 1441". Goldsmith's "revival" argument was subsequently adopted by the US.

Put simply – and it was by Goldsmith in nine, short bullet points – he argued that Security Council Resolution 678 had authorised the use of force to remove Iraq from Kuwait *and* "to restore international peace and security in the area"; that Resolution 687 established a ceasefire subject to conditions, particularly in relation to weapons inspections, thus suspending, but not terminating, the authority to use force in Resolution 678; that Iraq was in material breach of these conditions by its failure to provide a full accounting of its WMDs and to allow full and unimpeded access to international inspectors; that the Security Council had, in Resolution 1441, recognised these material breaches and warned against future material breaches, giving Iraq "a final opportunity to comply with its disarmament obligations" and warning of "serious consequences" if it did not; and that, material breaches having continued, the authority to use force in Resolution 678 had revived without the need for a further Security Council resolution.

Essentially, this justification depends upon a particular interpretation of Resolution 1441 – and therein lies its weakness. The Security Council did not explicitly authorise the use of force if its renewed demands were not met; nor did it implicitly do so. All it did was warn of serious consequences for further material breaches. The Security Council did not delegate to States the enforcement (by force or any other method) of its demands: it required further breaches to be reported to it by UNMOVIC and remained seized of the matter, clearly indicating that it intended to decide what action to take if further breaches occurred. During the adoption of Resolution 1441, the two principal sponsors, the US and UK, guaranteed that the resolution contained no "hidden triggers" or "automaticity" with respect to the use of force; and that any further breach of Iraq's disarmament obligations would be returned to the Council for appropriate action. For them then to found on a trigger in Resolution

1441 to revive automatically the authorisation in Resolution 678 is as disingenuous as it is dishonest.

Ten days before the Attorney-General's advice to the Cabinet, on 7 March 2003, he had provided a lengthy and nuanced "draft" to the Prime Minister. In this advice, understandably not made public until April 2005, Lord Goldsmith quickly dismissed, as legal justifications for the use of force in Iraq, self-defence (there being no armed attack or imminence of attack) and humanitarian intervention (being too controversial and, in any event, inappropriate to the circumstances); and he argued in detail the case for the authorisation of force by the Security Council through the revival of Resolution 678. But even here, he described the revival justification as no more than a "reasonably arguable case" and recommended that "the safest legal course would be to secure the adoption of a further resolution to authorise the use of force".

The clear conclusion is that, if the revival argument fails, as it must, there is no legal justification of the invasion of Iraq in 2003.

Essential Facts

- The first blanket prohibition on the use of force was introduced in 1945 by Art 2(4) of the UN Charter, that prohibition now being a peremptory norm of general international law.
- Force may be used by States in only two circumstances: in self-defence or as authorised by the Security Council.
- Self-defence requires an urgent necessity to response to an armed attack or imminent armed attack and a proportionate response to that necessity.
- While the Security Council has the power to use force, it invariably authorises States to act to restore international peace and security.

Essential Cases

Caroline Incident (1837): following an attack by British troops on an American vessel, correspondence between the US and UK set out the requirements for self-defence: there must be an urgent necessity to act and the action taken must be proportionate to the danger.

Military and Paramilitary Activities Case (1986): finding certain American activities in support of the Contra insurgents in Nicaragua in breach of international law, the ICJ held that the prohibition on the use of force was *jus cogens* and that self-defence required something approaching an armed attack.

Legality of the Threat or Use of Nuclear Weapons Case (1996): in an advisory opinion, the ICJ ruled that, in the present state of international law, the threat or use of nuclear weapons was not prohibited; and that they could be used as a last-resort measure when the very existence of a State was in jeopardy.

9 HUMAN RIGHTS

Human rights have become so much part of the international legal landscape that it is difficult to appreciate that, as a sub-discipline of international law, they date from only 1945. That is not to say that international law lacked humanitarian concern before then. The laws of war (discussed below), devised from the middle of the 19th century, were intended to make war more humane. After World War I, concerns for the well-being of religious and other minority groups in those European States being reconfigured in the peace treaties resulted in the conclusion of a number of minority treaties, guaranteeing rights to these groups. The customary rules on how a State treats foreign nationals were designed to secure for them a minimum international standard of treatment (see Chapter 7).

In the thinking of the first half of the 20th century, how a State treated its own nationals was accepted as being exclusively for it to determine; it was within its domestic jurisdiction. The Nazi atrocities immediately before and during World War II led to the realisation that it was futile to rely on States to respect the rights of their own nationals; many of the Nazi atrocities had been committed against German citizens who were, or at least should have been, protected by the guarantees in the German constitution. It was thought imperative to set some general and universal standards for the treatment by States of all people within their territory.

In their post-1945 manifestation, human rights are based on human dignity. In classifying human rights, it is common to refer to them as belonging to the civil and political or to the economic and social; or to generations, First Generation human rights being civil and political rights, Second Generation being economic and social rights and Third Generation being group rights (such as self-determination and the rights of indigenous peoples).

Human rights, very broadly defined, encompasses international human rights ("IHR"), the rules that emerged though treaties concluded after 1945 guaranteeing rights to all people within States; international humanitarian law ("IHL"), the rules formerly called the laws of war governing the conduct of armed conflicts; and international criminal law ("ICL"), the rules and fora governing the responsibility of individuals for crimes under international law.

INTERNATIONAL HUMAN RIGHTS

Globally

The term "human rights" does not appear in the discussions during the drafting of the UN Charter, though it is employed six times in the text of the Charter. In sum, the UN and its members committed themselves to promote universal respect for human rights and fundamental freedoms for all without distinction as to sex, race, language or religion, without specifying what human rights and fundamental freedoms were to be promoted. Pursuant to these obligations, the General Assembly established the Commission on Human Rights which, under the inspired leadership of Eleanor Roosevelt, drafted the Universal Declaration on Human Rights (UDHR). This seminal declaration, adopted by the General Assembly on 10 December 1948, is, according to its preamble, intended to be "a common standard of achievement for all peoples and all nations" – and so indeed it has turned out to be. In 30 short articles, it sets out the principal human rights to be accorded to all people in all countries.

Being nothing more than a General Assembly resolution, the UDHR is not legally binding and the Commission on Human Rights continued its work to create a binding international bill of rights, enshrined in treaty. Nonetheless, it is commonly accepted that some of the provisions of the UDHR have become part of customary law. Even the most cursory knowledge of how customary law is created dictates that the whole declaration cannot be custom and that only those parts that have come to be followed in State practice and to receive subsequent approval by repetition in treaties can be custom. One influential American authority, the American Law Institute, has suggested that the prohibition of genocide, slavery and the slave trade, torture or other cruel, inhuman, or degrading treatment or punishment are part of customary law, plus (with less confidence) killings or causing the disappearance of individuals, prolonged arbitrary detention, systematic racial discrimination and a consistent pattern of gross violations of internationally recognised human rights.

It took the Commission on Human Rights until 1966 to complete the international Bill of Rights by the elaboration of two international Conventions. For nearly two decades, the Commission had been debating whether there should be one or two Conventions; whether, if one, it should contain some monitoring or enforcement provisions; and, if two, whether one should deal with rights and the other with monitoring and enforcement. In the event, the Commission opted for an International Covenant on Civil and Political Rights and an International Covenant on Economic, Social and Cultural Rights, each expanding on the rights already set out in the UDHR and each containing its own system of monitoring and enforcement. These two covenants came into force in 1976, the year of the British ratification of both; the Civil and Political Rights Covenant presently has 165 parties, the Economic, Social and Cultural Rights Covenant 160 parties.

In addition, the Commission has been instrumental in the adoption of a number of other global human rights Conventions:

- Convention on the Elimination of All Forms of Racial Discrimination 1965;
- Convention on the Elimination of All Forms of Discrimination against Women 1979;
- Convention against Torture 1984;
- Convention on the Rights of the Child 1989;
- International Convention on the Protection of the Rights of All Migrant Workers and Members of Their Families 1990;
- Convention on the Rights of Person with Disabilities 2006.

With these Conventions, and others, and innumerable declarations from the General Assembly and international conferences, there is no shortage of substantive human rights norms. That said, everything bad perpetrated against individuals in a State and everything good desired by individuals cannot be a human right. Human rights are those rights that States have accepted as binding on them. It is, therefore, important to examine carefully the terms of any Convention to determine exactly what States have agreed to; to examine any limitations or qualifications contained in the stated rights; and to examine also any reservations made by States.

There has been much discussion over the years on whether all human rights are equal or whether there is some hierarchy of rights. While common sense may indicate that human rights constitute a hierarchy, the trend, particularly among human rights activists, is to regard all human rights as "universal, indivisible and interdependent and interrelated" to be treated "in a fair and equal manner, on the same footing and with the same emphasis": Vienna Declaration and Programme of Action on Human Rights 1993. There is consensus that some human rights are *jus cogens*, in the sense that they are accepted as fundamental and not capable of derogation. This limited group of rights corresponds with the rights thought also to be part of customary law: the prohibition on genocide, slavery and the slave trade, torture and unauthorised killings and disappearances. The difficulty is that, while there may be agreement that some human rights have the elevated status of *jus cogens*, there is no agreement as how far beyond these enumerated prohibitions the status extends.

The fundamental question from the outset had been how to ensure compliance by States with the standards contained in international human rights Conventions. The basic method of monitoring the obligations assumed by States involves regular reports by these States as to their implementation of their obligations contained in the relevant treaty, in particular the extent to which their law and practice conform to these obligations. These reports are then examined by some independent, and usually expert, committee appointed under the relevant treaty, which committee ultimately issues some concluding observations. The cycle of periodic reports, examination and concluding observations is part of the process of constructive dialogue, whereby States are prompted and encouraged to conform their law and practice to the international standards they have accepted.

This relatively light-touch compliance method falls to be contrasted with the more intrusive complaints procedure, whereby States accept the right of another State, and exceptionally individuals, to complain to an independent committee concerning violations of obligations under the relevant treaty. This committee then examines the complaint and ultimately issues a quasi-judicial determination.

The Civil and Political Rights Covenant, containing long-established civil liberties and requiring little of States other than that they do not violate them, included a reports *and* a complaints compliance regime. The Covenant itself allowed a State to complain about violations by another State, provided the State complained against had accepted this possibility; and, in an Optional Protocol, also of 1966, individuals were, subject to some conditions, given the right to complain against their own Government. The Economic, Social and Cultural Rights Covenant, containing relatively new rights and requiring positive action on the part of States, included only a reports regime. The early trend became to have reports for all global human rights Conventions and complaints for only those with hard civil liberties-style rights. The more recent trend is to have a complaints regime for all; at this time, only the Economic, Social and Cultural Rights Covenant and the Convention on the Rights of the Child (and this is in the process of change) make no provision for complaints by individuals.

Regionally

Alongside this global activity through the United Nations, there are a number of regional human rights agreements. There is a human rights regime for the Americas and for Africa, but the most famous human rights regime exists in Europe under the European Convention on Human Rights of 1950. The European Convention was adopted through the Council of Europe, an international organisation established in 1949 as a political bulwark against communism, which has 47 parties, including now the European States that formerly were part of the Soviet empire.

The European Convention contains a fairly standard enumeration of civil and political rights; these substantive rights have been added to by six protocols. What marks the Convention out is its sophisticated (for the time and even now) arrangements to ensure State compliance. Individual complaints have been part of the European system from the outset, and in revised arrangements, enacted by Protocol No 11 of 1994, the European Court of Human Rights has jurisdiction to hear complaints brought by individuals subject to very minimal conditions: that the complain is not frivolous and that all remedies in the State complained against have been exhausted. The European Court of Human Rights has been a victim of its own success, being overwhelmed by individual complaints from an increased number of States parties, leading to long delays in deciding cases. Ironically, the streamlining of the Court's procedure in 1994 has contributed to these delays; equally ironically, the Court's jurisprudence is replete with condemnations of delays in court proceedings within States. Further reforms, involving further streamlining of the Court's procedure and contained in Protocol 14 of 2004, have been accepted by all States Parties, except Russia.

Four cases of importance have reached the European Court of Human Rights from Scotland. In *Campbell and Cosans* v *UK* (1982), when two parents objected to the use of corporal punishment in their sons' schools, the Court held that, while corporal punishment was not a violation of Art 3 (prohibition of torture) as neither boy had been so punished, it was a violation of Art 2 (right to education) of Protocol 1 of 1952 in that the UK had failed to ensure respect for the parents' philosophical convictions. This case was an important cog in the process, much of it conducted under the European Convention on Human Rights, whereby corporal punishment was abolished in all State-supported schools in 1987 and in private schools in 1999. In *Campbell* v *UK* (1993), it was held that interference by opening and reading correspondence between a prisoner serving a life sentence for murder and his solicitor was a violation of Art 8 (right to respect for private and family life); as a consequence of the decision, the Prison Rules were amended to ensure confidentiality in correspondence between prisoners and their lawyers.

McMichael v *UK* (1995) is most famous for the insistence by the European Court that the minimum standards set out in Art 6 (right to a fair trial) applied to the informal children's hearings system, particularly by requiring disclosure to the family of all reports made available to the hearing; and the Children's Hearings (Scotland) Rules were amended to accommodate the Court's ruling. In *X* v *UK* (2002), when four children complained that they had been exposed to sexual abuse by their mother's cohabitant, the Court held that the UK was in breach of Art 3 in that the relevant organ of local government had failed to investigate allegations of sexual abuse.

INTERNATIONAL HUMANITARIAN LAW

International humanitarian law is the term employed to describe the rules of international law especially designed for the protection of the individual in time of war or armed conflict. It is a major part of the laws of war (*jus in bello*), the rules governing the conduct of armed conflict. Rules on the conduct of hostilities first emerged in the middle of the 19th century, originally as (enlightened) instructions by States to their armies in the field, which were ultimately enshrined in treaties and other instruments adopted at The Hague in 1899 and 1907 and at Geneva in 1929.

The principal instruments today are the four Conventions adopted at Geneva on 12 August 1949:

i.   Convention for the Amelioration of the Condition of the Wounded and Sick in Armed Forces in the Field;

ii. Convention for the Amelioration of the Condition of Wounded, Sick and Shipwrecked Members of Armed Forces at Sea;

iii. Convention relative to the Treatment of Prisoners of War; and

iv. Convention relative to the Protection of Civilian Persons in Time of War.

In 1977, two Protocols to the 1949 Geneva Conventions were adopted:

i.   Relating to the Protection of Victims of International Armed Conflicts; and

ii. Relating to the Protection of Victims of Non-International Armed Conflicts.

The Red Cross has published seven Fundamental Rules of International Humanitarian Law in Armed Conflicts. While these rules have no official or legal status, they are excellent distillations of the principles in the four Geneva Conventions, the two Protocols and the relevant customary law. They are instructive as a comprehensive and intelligible articulation of international humanitarian law:

1. Persons *hors de combat* and those who do not take a direct part in hostilities are entitled to respect for their lives and physical and moral integrity. They shall in all circumstances be protected and treated humanely without any adverse distinction.

2. It is forbidden to kill or injure an enemy who surrenders or who is *hors de combat*.

3. The wounded and sick shall be collected and cared for by the party to the conflict which has them in its power. Protection also covers medical personnel, establishments, transports and *materiel*. The emblem of the red cross (red crescent, red lion and sun) is the sign of such protection and must be respected.

4. Captured combatants and civilians under the authority of an adverse party are entitled to respect for their lives, dignity, personal rights and convictions. They shall be protected against all acts of violence and reprisals. They shall have the right to correspond with their families and to receive relief.

5. Everyone shall be entitled to benefit from fundamental judicial guarantees. No one shall be responsible for an act he has not committed. No one shall be subjected to physical or mental torture, corporal punishment or cruel or degrading treatment.

6. Parties to a conflict and members of their armed forces do not have an unlimited choice of methods and means of warfare. It is prohibited to employ weapons or methods of warfare of a nature to cause unnecessary losses or excessive suffering.

7. Parties to a conflict shall at all times distinguish between the civilian population and combatants in order to spare civilian population and property. Neither the civilian population nor civilian persons shall be the object of attack. Attacks shall be directed solely against military objectives.

INTERNATIONAL CRIMINAL LAW

Like international human rights themselves, international criminal law, as we know it today, is essentially a product of the immediate post-World War II era. Much of its development can be traced to the International

Military Tribunal established by the victorious Allies in 1945 to try the major German war criminals. At Nuremberg, between November 1945 and August 1946, 24 individuals and eight organisations were charged with a variety of crimes ranging from crimes against peace and war crimes to crimes against humanity; the Tribunal of four judges representing the principal Allies found 20 of the defendants guilty of one or more charges, of whom 12 were sentenced to death and the remainder to imprisonment for life or a term of years; one committed suicide during the trial and three were acquitted.

This momentous trial held, most importantly, that individuals could be held criminally responsible for crimes defined by international law. As the Tribunal said, "Crimes against international law are committed by men, not by abstract entities, and only by punishing individuals who commit such crimes can the provisions of international law be enforced". The Nuremberg Principles of 1950, drawing on the Statute of the Tribunal and its judgment and approved by the General Assembly, have been the basis of all subsequent international criminal law, establishing not only that individuals are legally responsible for international crimes, but also that there is no immunity for those in high Government positions, that superior orders are no defence, that complicity is equally an international crime and that any person charged with an international crime has the right to a fair trial.

The distinguishing feature of international criminal law is that it attaches criminal liability to individuals, usually though the medium of national courts, but increasingly through international criminal tribunals.

Substantive international criminal law

The very earliest international crime was piracy, over which all States have jurisdiction. From the mid-19th century, it was recognised that individuals committing war crimes were liable to prosecution by the authorities of their own State, war crimes being grave breaches of the laws and customs of war. From the early 20th century, States began to co-operate in the suppression of crimes of common concern, such as slavery and slave trading and drugs and people trafficking (this last phenomenon being described by the unfortunate term "white slavery" in the relevant treaties of the time).

The Nuremberg Principles defined three crimes in broad terms: crimes against peace; war crimes, being "violations of the laws and customs of war"; and crimes against humanity, being "murder, extermination, enslavement, deportation and other inhuman acts done against any civilian population, or persecutions on political, racial or religious grounds, when such acts are done or such persecutions are carried on in execution of or in connection with any crime against peace or any war crime". These are now the core crimes of ICL.

The best modern articulation of substantive ICL is contained in the Statute of the International Criminal Court, Art 5 of which lists four international crimes: genocide; crimes against humanity; war crimes; and the crime of aggression. Following the definition set out in the Genocide Convention of 1948, genocide is constituted by a number of specified acts intended "to destroy, in whole or in part, a national, ethnical, racial or religious group" (Art 6). Crimes against humanity are specified acts, including murder, enslavement, torture, rape and enforced disappearance, "committed as part of a widespread or systematic attack directed against any civilian population, with knowledge of the attack" (Art 7(1)). War crimes are defined as grave breaches of the Geneva Conventions of 12 August 1949 (Art 8(2)).

Adjective international criminal law

The common feature of early international crimes (piracy, slave trading, drugs and people trafficking) was that the prosecution was left to municipal authorities in municipal courts. States were prepared to accept a common definition of these crimes and co-operation in their suppression, but they would not concede that there should be any kind of international prosecution and adjudication. Jurisdiction over crime was – and still is – regarded as such an important aspect of a State's sovereignty that the its surrender to an international forum is problematical. The Nuremberg trials broke the mould: for the first time, individuals who had committed offences which would have been before municipal courts (such as murder, rape, torture and war crimes) were brought before an international tribunal.

Further encouragement for those anxious to see a permanent international criminal court was given by the 1948 Genocide Convention, which provided in Art VI that those charged with genocide should be tried in a municipal tribunal or "such international penal tribunal as may have jurisdiction", though no such tribunal existed at the time – indeed, no such tribunal existed until the creation of the ICC in 1998.

International concern about terrorism has resulted in resulted in the conclusion of a total of 13 Conventions, ranging in subject-matter from the hijacking and sabotage of aircraft to terrorist bombings and nuclear terrorism, all of which are predicated on municipal, and not international, prosecution and trial. Terrorist crimes were deliberately excluded from the jurisdiction of the ICC because there already existed a self-contained "sectoral" regime, a decision that seems at odds with the post 9/11 determination to fight a "war on terror".

The movement to create an international criminal court gained momentum with the creation by the UN Security Council of two *ad hoc* tribunals: the International Criminal Tribunal for the Former Yugoslavia (ICTY) and the International Criminal Court for Rwanda (ICTR), each with jurisdiction over war crimes, genocide and crimes against humanity. While these two tribunals proved controversial, cumbersome and expensive, they did demonstrate the possibilities of international criminal adjudication; and their rules and procedures have provided a model for the ICC.

That court was created, after considerable discussion, by the Statute of the International Criminal Court, concluded at Rome in 1998; the Statute entered into force in 2002 and has 110 States Parties, significantly excluding the US. Under Art 5 of the Statute, the ICC has jurisdiction over genocide, war crimes and crimes against humanity; and will have jurisdiction over the "crime of aggression" once that crime has an agreed definition. It has jurisdiction only over crimes committed after the entry into force of the Statute in 2002 (Art 11). The Court can exercise jurisdiction over crimes committed on the territory of a State Party, including on board a ship or aircraft registered to a State Party, and in respect of crimes committed by a national of a State Party (Art 12). Alleged crimes may be referred to the prosecutor by a State Party or by the UN Security Council; alternatively, prosecutions may be initiated by the prosecutor *ex proprio motu* (Art 13).

The jurisdiction of the ICC is "complementary to national criminal jurisdictions" (Art 1). This basic principle of complementarity is given substance by Art 17, effectively declaring that the ICC has no jurisdiction where a case is being investigated and prosecuted by a State with jurisdiction or where a decision has been made by a State not to prosecute as long as that State was able and willing to carry out an investigation or prosecution.

There is an increasing trend towards using international criminal tribunals comprising local and international judges and applying local and international criminal law, referred to as hybrid tribunals. Among the clearest examples of hybrids are the Lebanon Special Tribunal, the Extraordinary Chambers in the Courts of Cambodia and the Special Court for Sierra Leone. All three were established pursuant to an agreement between the United Nations and the State concerned; all dealt with matters that had attracted serious international concern or involved international crimes; all required domestic and international judges (and prosecutors) to be appointed jointly by the UN and the State concerned; all have a statute, specifying the procedure and rules of evidence, contained in the agreements with the UN; and all have imported into their proceedings recognised standards of international due process. On this analysis, the Scottish Court in the Netherlands that heard the Lockerbie trial and the Iraqi High Tribunal that tried Saddam Hussein do not qualify as hybrids, both being more accurately regarded as internationalised domestic courts or tribunals.

Essential Facts

- International human rights are the product of declarations and treaties, all dating from 1945, the most important of which remains the 1948 Universal Declaration of Human Rights.
- Many particular human rights articulated in treaties, such as the prohibitions on torture, genocide and slavery, have become peremptory norms of general international law.
- International humanitarian law, dating from the mid-19th century, is concerned with ameliorating the hardships of armed conflict, originally for the combatants and increasingly now for civilians.
- International criminal law derives from the Nuremberg trials; and, after nearly 50 years in gestation, there is now a permanent International Criminal Court.

Essential Cases

Nuremberg Trials (1945–46): for the first time, an international tribunal tried senior military and civilian leaders of a country for crimes against peace, war crimes and crimes of humanity, holding individuals liable for international crimes.

Campbell and Cosans v UK (1982): a Scottish case before the European Court of Human Rights held that corporal punishment in schools was impermissible as being contrary to the parents' philosophical convictions and led to the eventual abolition of all corporal punishment in schools.

10 LAW OF THE SEA

The law of the sea is that body of rules of law governing the uses to which the sea, constituting 70 per cent of the earth's surface area, may be put. These rules, many of long standing, emerged from the practice of States, particularly from the maritime practice of the UK during the years of its naval ascendency in the 18th and 19th centuries. Because of the notorious vagueness of custom and the desire to have clarity and certainty in this important area, the law of the sea was thought to be an ideal early candidate for codification.

CODIFICATION

The first significant attempt to codify the customary rules of international law on the sea occurred at the League of Nations Conference for the Codification of International Law in 1930, which considered the question of the territorial sea. While no definitive agreement was reached, State practice and attitudes concerning the territorial sea were explored. The First United Nations Conference on the Law of the Sea met in Geneva from February to April 1958 and, basing its work on drafts submitted by the International Law Commission, adopted four Conventions, on the Territorial Sea and the Contiguous Zone, the High Seas, Fishing and the Conservation of the Living Resources of the High Seas and the Continental Shelf. The Second United Nations Conference on the Law of the Sea (UNCLOS II) met in Geneva in 1960, but could reach no agreement on the issues before it: the breadth of the territorial sea and fishing limits.

The Third United Nations Conference on the Law of the Sea (UNCLOS III) met first, for an organisational session, in New York, in December 1973, thereafter in substantive sessions in Caracas, Geneva and New York from June 1974. On 30 April 1982, the UN Convention on the Law of the Sea was signed at Montego Bay, Jamaica. The Convention is huge, with 320 articles and eleven annexes. Part XI (on the regime for deep-sea mining) was subsequently amended in 1994 by the Agreement relating to the Implementation of Part XI of the UN Convention on the Law of the Sea. There are 160 parties to the Convention and 138 parties to the 1994 Agreement.

BASELINES

Baselines are the lines from which the breadth of the territorial sea and the other maritime zones is measured, "the normal baseline", according to Art 5 of the UN Convention on the Law of the Sea, being "the low-water line along the coast as marked on large-scale charts officially recognized by the coastal State". Article 7(1) provides that:

> "In localities where the coastline is deeply indented and cut into, or if there is a fringe of islands along the coast in its immediate vicinity, the method of straight baselines joining appropriate points may be employed in drawing the baseline from which the breadth of the territorial sea is measured."

Straight baselines may not depart to any appreciable extent from the general direction of the coast, and the sea areas lying within the line must be sufficiently closely linked to the land domain to be subject to the regime of internal waters; and account may be taken of peculiar economic interests in the determination of particular baselines. These criteria for drawing straight baselines are taken virtually unchanged from the *Anglo–Norwegian Fisheries Case* (1951), in which the ICJ accepted the Norwegian practice of drawing straight baselines across the mouths of fjords and along fringing islands, islets and rocks just off its coastline (the *skjærgaard*) as "imposed by the peculiar geography of the Norwegian coast". While there is no limit on the length of straight baselines, a straight baseline across the mouth of a bay, referred to as a closing line, can be no longer than 24 miles (Art 10). Waters on the landward side of the baselines are internal waters and fall within the exclusive sovereignty of the coastal State.

TERRITORIAL SEA

It had long been recognised in international law that a coastal State has authority over a belt of water adjacent to its coast, generally termed the territorial sea or territorial waters. According to the Dutch scholar Cornelius van Bynkershoek, a State could claim jurisdiction within the range of its shore batteries, often referred to as the "cannon-shot rule". By the end of the 18th century, the range of artillery was about 3 miles or 1 marine league and that distance became generally recognised as the breadth of the territorial sea. However, attempts to fix a limit failed of agreement at the League of Nations Codification Conference in 1930, at UNCLOS I in 1958 and UNCLOS II in 1960. Increasing State claims to a territorial sea of 12 miles are recognised in Art 3 of the UN Convention on the Law of the Sea: "Every State has the right to establish the breadth of its territorial sea up to a limit not exceeding 12 nautical miles ...".

Until relatively recently, there was some confusion as to the nature of a State's rights in the territorial sea – were they sovereign rights, proprietary rights or merely rights of jurisdiction and control? This confusion was highlighted in the *Franconia Case* (1876), where the question arose as to whether the master of the *Franconia* was amenable to the courts of England for manslaughter for his role in the collision in the territorial sea off Dover with the British vessel *Strathclyde*, resulting in the loss of one life. In deciding by 7 to 6 that the English courts had no jurisdiction over Captain Keyn without empowering legislation (and there was none), a total of 10 judges gave opinions, from which it is almost impossible to identify a *ratio* as to the nature of a State's rights in its territorial sea.

According to Art 2 of the UN Convention on the Law of the Sea, the sovereignty of the coastal State extends to its territorial sea, but that sovereignty is exercised subject to conventional and other rules of international law; the sovereignty of the coastal State extends also to the airspace above, and the sea-bed below, the territorial sea. There are two principal restrictions on a coastal State's sovereignty in its territorial sea: jurisdiction in the territorial sea and the right of foreign vessels to innocent passage.

The question of jurisdiction is the territorial sea, the nub of the *Franconia Case*, is provided for in Arts 27 and 28 of the UN Convention. A coastal State "should not" (not "must not") exercise criminal jurisdiction on board a foreign vessel in its territorial sea except where the consequences of the crime extend to the coastal State or where the crime is of a kind "to disturb the peace of the country or the of the territorial sea". In relation to civil jurisdiction, it too "should not" be exercised by a coastal State over a foreign vessel passing through its territorial sea.

The right of innocent passage is a long-established rule of international law. The UN Convention on the Law of the Sea sets down detailed rules on innocent passage, commencing with the general principles that "ships of all States, whether coastal or land-locked, shall enjoy the right of innocent passage through the territorial sea" (Art 17) and that "[t]he coastal State must not hamper innocent passage through the territorial sea" (Art 24(1)). For the purposes of this right, "passage" means movement that must be "continuous and expeditious", though it may include "stopping and anchoring, but only in so far as they are incidental to ordinary navigation or are rendered necessary by *force majeure* or by distress" (Art 18(2)).

According to Art 19(1), "[p]assage is innocent so long as it is not prejudicial to the peace, good order or security of the coastal State. Such passage shall take place in conformity with this Convention and with other rules of international law". There then follows (in Art 19(2)) a list of 12 categories of activity that are not to be considered as innocent, including any exercise or practice of weapons, any act of propaganda or information collection and any act of wilful and serious pollution. All foreign vessels exercising the right of innocent passage must observe the laws and regulations, particularly those relating to transport and navigation (Art 21).

The UN Convention, like its predecessor the Geneva Convention on the Territorial Sea of 1958, is not wholly clear as to whether warships enjoy the right of innocent passage. Certainly, in the *Corfu Channel Case* (1949), the ICJ held that British warships had the right to pass freely through the Corfu Channel, located wholly within Albanian territorial waters. While some States accord warships the right of innocent passage through their territorial sea, about 40 States allow the entry of warships into the territorial sea only with permission or after notification.

CONTIGUOUS ZONE

At the time when the breadth of the territorial sea was narrow, States began to exercise preventive or protective control for certain purposes over a belt of high sea contiguous to their territorial sea, and a limited contiguous zone jurisdiction was recognised in customary law. This jurisdiction is now regulated by Art 33 of the UN Convention on the Law of the Sea:

> "(1) In a zone contiguous to its territorial sea, described as the contiguous zone, the coastal State may exercise the control necessary to: (a) prevent infringement of its customs, fiscal, immigration or sanitary regulations within its territory or territorial sea; (b) punish infringement of the above regulations committed within its territory or territorial sea.
>
> (2) The contiguous zone may not extend beyond 24 nautical miles from the baselines from which the breadth of the territorial sea is measured."

CONTINENTAL SHELF

States began to make claims to the hydrocarbon resources in the sea-bed off their coasts in the 1940s. While States clearly had the right to these resources in the sea-bed of their territorial sea, the claims went further in asserting rights in the sea-bed of the high sea. The question then arose as to whether a State could claim an exclusive hydrocarbons zone in the high sea when it could not claim an exclusive fishing zone in the high sea. In the early 1950s, it is clear that there was no right under customary international law for any State to claim continental shelf rights. The arbiter in the *Abu Dhabi Arbitration* (1951) described the continental shelf doctrine as lacking "definitive status" because of "so many ragged ends and unfilled blanks, and so much that is merely tentative and exploratory".

In the 1950s, the ILC drafted, and UNCLOS I adopted, a short (15 articles, of which only seven are substantive) Convention on the Continental Shelf. By 1969, the ICJ ruled that the main provisions of the Geneva Convention of 1958 reflected customary law: *North Sea Continental Shelf Cases* (1969). The relevant law on the continental shelf is now contained in the UN Convention on the Law of the Sea.

Article 76(1) defines the extent of the continental shelf as "the seabed and subsoil of the submarine areas that extend beyond its territorial sea throughout the natural prolongation of its land territory to the outer edge of the continental margin, or to a distance of 200 nautical miles from the baselines from which the breadth of the territorial sea is measured where the outer edge of the continental margin does not extend up to that distance". Article 76 goes on to establish a complicated formula for determining the outer edge of the continental margin, setting an absolute outer limit at 350 miles from the baselines of the territorial sea or 100 miles from the 2,500-metre isobath. For those States claiming beyond 200 miles (referred to as "margin claims"), a Commission on the Limits of the Continental Shelf was established to consider these claims; its recommendations are to be regarded as final and binding in determine the outer edge of a margin claim. Where a State claims beyond 200 miles (to the outer edge of the continental margin), it must make either payments or contributions in kind to the international community in respect of the resources exploited beyond the 200 miles line (Art 82).

Within the continental shelf thus defined, the coastal State has "sovereign rights for the purpose of exploring it and exploiting its natural resources" (Art 77(1)), these rights not being of sovereignty, but rather of jurisdiction and control. These rights are exclusive to the coastal State, and do not depend on any claim or proclamation by the coastal State; and they do not affect the status of the superjacent waters. The natural resources to which the coastal State is entitled are the "mineral and other non-living of the seabed and subsoil together with living organisms belonging to sedentary species ..." (Art 77(4)). The coastal State is entitled to establish on its continental shelf artificial island, installations and structures, with safety zones of 500 metres around them.

Considerable difficulty and controversy have surrounded the legal rules for delimiting the boundary of the continental shelf between opposite and adjacent States. The formula in Art 6 of the 1958 Geneva Convention, the so-called "equidistance-special circumstances rule" (ie that, in the absence of special circumstances justifying another boundary, the boundary should be the median or equidistance line), was held in the *North Sea Continental Shelf Cases* (1969) not to represent customary law. As a consequence, the ICJ had to identify the appropriate customary rule. Ignoring the fact that there were 15 cited applications of the equidistance/ special circumstances formula, indicating that what practice there was supported the formula, the Court devised a rule for which there was no support in the practice of States. This formula is vague in the extreme: that delimitation is to achieve an equitable solution taking account of all relevant circumstances. While these apparently quite different formulae might well have the same object and effect (*Anglo–French Continental Shelf Case* (1978), the customary test has come to prevail. Article 83(1) of the UN Convention promulgates a clumsy, unintelligible and unhelpful compromise between the two tests: "The delimitation of the continental shelf between States with opposite or adjacent coasts shall be effected by agreement on the basis of international law, as referred to in Article 38 of the Statute of the International Court of Justice, in order to achieve an equitable solution."

EXCLUSIVE ECONOMIC ZONE

The exclusive economic zone (EEZ) is a concept developed at UNCLOS III, and was intended to accord to every coastal State exclusive jurisdiction and control over the natural resources of the sea-bed, sub-soil and superjacent waters off its coast to a distance of 200 miles. The EEZ was derived from, and was intended as a merger of, two concepts: the continental shelf and the exclusive fishery zone.

The extent of State control over fishing off its coast had been problematic for a long time. Up till the middle of the 20th century, all that could be said with certainty was that a State's exclusive right to regulate fishing extended throughout its territorial sea; beyond that, fishing was a freedom of the high sea and open to the vessels of all States. From the 1960s, States began to make claims to extensive fishing zones, some of up to 200 miles from the coast, in which they asserted the exclusive right to regulate fishing. In the *Fisheries Jurisdiction Cases* ((1974) 175), the ICJ, holding that Iceland could not enforce a 50-mile exclusive fishing zone against the UK and West Germany because their fishermen had historic rights to fish in the area, declined to rule on what would be the legitimate extent of a State's fishing zone. This seems unduly cautious, as, at the time of the ruling, many States were already claiming a 200-mile exclusive zone and it was clear that UNCLOS III would enact a 200-mile all-resource zone. It was generally accepted that, by the late 1970s, a State could claim an exclusive fishing zone of 200 miles as part of customary law.

The intention at UNCLOS III to establish an all-resource zone of 200 miles, forging the continental shelf and the exclusive fishing zone into an EEZ, did not quite happen. While the rights of coastal and other States in the continental shelf and the EEZ are essentially the same, the extent of the zones differs. In relation to fishing, the extent of the EEZ is 200 miles (Art 57 of the UN Convention); in relation to the continental shelf, the zone may extend beyond 200 miles to the outer edge of the continental margin.

According to Art 56(1), the coastal State's rights in the EEZ are "sovereign rights for the purpose of exploring and exploiting, conserving and managing the natural resources ... and with regard to other activities for the economic exploitation and exploration of the zone, such as the production of energy from the water, currents and winds". The Convention, in Arts 61–62, requires each coastal State to determine the maximum sustainable yield for each species using the best available scientific evidence, to identify the capacity of its fishermen to harvest the fish within this total allowable catch and to afford other States access to any surplus fish stocks, special regard being had to allowing access to fishermen from developing States and States that have traditionally fished in the area.

HIGH SEA

While we now have a clear idea of the various maritime zones and the rights of coastal and other States in these zones, this was not always the case. The blame, if blame there be absent consensus among States as to these zones and the rights in them, begins with the famous "battle of the books". These books were nothing more than propaganda on behalf of particular European States and their maritime interests dressed up in legal verbiage. On behalf of the Netherlands and their attempts to intrude on Portugal's claimed monopoly in the East Indies, and Portugal's consequent claim to exclude foreign vessels from the surrounding seas, Grotius argued for the complete freedom of the seas in his open seas doctrine. The essence of Grotius's thesis, first advanced in 1609 in *Mare*

Liberum, was that "[t]he sea is common to all because it is so limitless that it cannot become a possession of any one, and because it is adapted for the use of all, whether we consider it from the point of view of navigation or of fisheries".

The battle was joined by scholars from other States, the most formidable of whom was John Selden, writing in support of the attempts by the British Crown to require licences of foreign fishermen wishing access to "English" waters. In *Mare Clausum* (1625), he gave a masterly exposition of the English assertion, basing his argument on principle and precedent. Selden may have won the intellectual battle, but Grotius won the war: it did not take long for the *mare liberum* principle to prevail in the practice of States in relation to the high sea. But, in another sense, both won, because Selden had vehemently argued for, and Grotius had conceded, a zone of exclusive State control abutting the coast – what we now think of as the territorial sea.

The traditional definition of the high sea is reflected in Art 1 of the 1958 Geneva Convention on the High Seas as "all parts of the sea that are not included in the territorial sea or the internal waters of a State". Article 86 of the UN Convention on the Law of the Sea redefines the high sea as "all parts of the sea that are not included in the exclusive economic zone, in the territorial sea or in the internal waters of a State ...", while maintaining the freedoms for all States of navigation, overflight and laying of submarine cables and pipelines in the exclusive economic zone (Art 58(1)).

A basic freedom of navigation on the high sea, first argued for by Grotius, was established by the end of the 18th century. By the time of the UN Convention on the Law of the Sea, the term "freedom of the sea" embraced more than navigation. In terms of Art 87(1), it comprises, *inter alia*, freedom of navigation, of overflight, to lay submarine cables and pipelines, to construct artificial islands and other installations permitted under international law, of fishing, and to conduct scientific research.

International law has long regulated jurisdiction over vessels on the high seas, the basic principle being that "jurisdiction follows the flag". To that end, while every State has the right to grant its nationality (and thereby its flag) to ships, there must exist a genuine link between the State and the ship (Art 91(1) of the UN Convention). To bolster the genuine link requirement, Art 94(1) requires that "every State shall exercise its jurisdiction and control in administrative, technical and social matters over ships flying its flag"; and then proceeds to set out a number of specific and demanding duties in satisfaction of this effective jurisdiction and control. On the high seas, except as otherwise provided in the UN Convention or other treaties, ships are subject to the exclusive jurisdiction of the flag State (Art 92(1)).

It is estimated that something like 50 per cent (by tonnage) of the world's merchant fleet sails under the flags of States with which they have no genuine link, generally referred to as "flags of convenience". It was thought that the genuine link requirement, first set out in the 1958 High Seas Convention, would end "open registries" (the term used to describe those States granting flags of convenience) as they would be unable to exercise the necessary jurisdiction and control in administrative, technical and social matters. When that did not prove to be the case – indeed when the number of flags of convenience vessels increased – Art 94's list of duties pursuant to effective jurisdiction and control was thought to be enough to end the perceived scourge of flags of convenience. Again, that did not prove to be the case, largely because ship-owners have continued to register vessels in States with light-touch conditions, thereby reducing their operating costs, particularly in relation to the crew. While this might be objectionable to seamen's unions in developed States, where the wages and social benefits are high, there is no evidence for the belief that all flags of convenience vessels are rust buckets, crewed by incompetent drunks, with no charts or navigational equipment, and ever prone to collisions and other mishaps.

As an exception to the "jurisdiction follows the flag" rule, those responsible for piracy are subject to the jurisdiction of any State. In early times, piracy was so disruptive of safety at sea and international trade that universal jurisdiction over the perpetrators was justified as they were enemies of all humankind: *hostes humani generis*. The golden age of piracy may be over, but it remains a real and increasing problem today. Attacks on ships, particularly in the Red Sea and Indian Ocean, mainly by Somalia-based pirates, and in south East Asia, in the Straits of Malacca and around Singapore, are estimated to cost international shipping $15 million a year.

Article 101(1) of the UN Convention defines piracy as "any illegal acts of violence, detention or any act of depradation, committed for private ends by the crew or passengers of a private ship or a private aircraft" and directed against another ship or aircraft on the high seas. As to jurisdiction over pirates, Art 105 of the UN Convention provides that:

> "on the high seas, or in any other place outside the jurisdiction of any State, every State may seize a pirate ship or aircraft, or a ship taken by

piracy and under the control of pirates, and arrest the persons and seize the property on board. The courts of the State which carried out the seizure may decide upon the penalties to be imposed, and may also determine the action to be taken with regard to the ships, aircraft or property, subject to the rights of third parties acting in good faith".

Another exception to the "jurisdiction follows the flag" rule is the right of hot pursuit, enshrined now in Art 111 of the UN Convention, allowing enforcement vessels of a coastal State to pursue on to the high seas and seize a foreign merchant vessel that has offended against the State's laws. Such pursuit must be begun while the vessel is still in the State's territorial waters by a "visual or auditory order to stop", it must be continuous and uninterrupted and it must end when the pursued vessel enters the territorial sea of any other State. In the *I'm Alone Case* (1933–35), during prohibition in the US, a British rum-runner of Canadian registry was sunk on the high sea after it had refused to stop by the American sister ship of the original coastguard vessel that had begun the pursuit. Doubting that this was hot pursuit at all, the tribunal stated that the intentional sinking of the vessel went beyond the exercise of necessary and reasonable force for the purpose of her apprehension. There is no basis, absent a permissive treaty provision, for the extension of the maritime doctrine of hot pursuit to the pursuit of fugitives by a State's military forces across a frontier into a neighbouring State.

INTERNATIONAL SEABED AREA

International concern over the exploitation of the hard minerals, in particular manganese nodules, on the sea-bed and ocean floor beyond the limits of national jurisdiction (ie beyond the continental shelf) was first articulated in the UN General Assembly in 1967. Deep-sea mining was one of the central, and most controversial, issues at UNCLOS III.

Despite the international determination to declare the area beyond national jurisdiction, and its minerals, to be the common heritage of humankind and not subject to national appropriation or exploitation, and to devise an international regime to exploit the resources, some States declined to ratify the UN Convention on the Law of the Sea because of the provisions on deep-sea mining. Some few enacted legislation providing for the licensing and control of deep-sea mining by their nationals (see the Deep Sea Mining (Temporary Provisions) Act 1981 and the (US) Deep Sea-bed Hard Minerals Resources Act 1980).

According to Art 1(1) of the UN Convention, the international seabed area is "the seabed and ocean floor and subsoil thereof, beyond the limits of national jurisdiction". It is "the common heritage of mankind" (Art 136), not subject to appropriation by States, and its resources "are vested in mankind as a whole", on whose behalf the International Seabed Authority is to act (Art 137). The limits of national jurisdiction are the outer edge of the continental shelf, being 200 miles or the foot of the continental margin under Art 76 of the Convention.

The difficulties encountered at UNCLOS III, and inherent in Part XI of the UN Convention, concerned the accommodation between two almost irreconcilable views. The majority of States insisted that all mining be conducted directly by, and on behalf of, the international community, through an operating arm called the Enterprise under the aegis of a new international organisation, the International Seabed Authority. The minority, a group of States supporting the US, demanded that mining be conducted by corporations, subject at most to supervision by the ISA. The scheme adopted in the UN Convention attempted a compromise: exploration would be open to licensed corporations, and licences for exploitation would be granted to corporations conditional on the splitting of any licensed site with the Enterprise, the transfer of technology from the licensed corporation to the Enterprise and, in a complicated formula, the payment of annual fees and a percentage of the market value of the recovered minerals to the ISA.

To secure a workable regime for deep-sea mining, it was necessary to amend Pt XI of the UN Convention, and that was done in 1994 by the Agreement relating to the Implementation of Pt XI of the UN Convention on the Law of the Sea. This unusual agreement, which substantially recasts some of the provisions of Pt XI, is to be read as an integral part of the UN Convention for the parties to it (Art 1(2)) and, indeed, is to prevail over inconsistencies with the Convention (Art 2(1)). It addresses many of the concerns of the those States opposed to the original mining scheme, even the US, which ratified the Agreement, but still not the UN Convention itself, in 1996; the UK ratified both in 1997.

The original impetus for deep-sea mining was on nodules, often called manganese nodules, scattered on the deep-sea bed and ocean floor, and containing, in addition to manganese, copper, cobalt, zinc and even gold and silver. More recent interest has focused on hydrothermal vents, which create sulphide deposits containing the same range of minerals. However, commercial activity – and the legal and political controversies about deep-sea mining – has languished, largely because of the relatively cheap and ready supply of the same minerals from land-based sources.

Essential Facts

- The law of the sea can be viewed through a series maritime zones, with the extent of the coastal State's authority diminishing as the zones proceed further seaward.
- In its territorial sea of 12 miles, a coastal State has qualified sovereignty, the principal qualifications being the right of innocent passage and limited jurisdictional competence.
- A coastal State has only limited enforcement jurisdiction in its contiguous zone extending from 12 to 24 miles from its coast.
- Within its exclusive economic zone of 200 miles, a coastal State has the exclusive authority to conserve and manage the fish stocks.
- Within its continental shelf of at least 200 miles, a coastal State has exclusive authority over the oil and gas resources.
- Following the teachings of Grotius, all States enjoy the freedoms associated with the high sea, being that part of the oceans beyond the 200-mile resource zone allocated to States.
- The arrangements for mining the mineral resources of the international seabed area outside national jurisdiction, the common heritage of humankind, have proved difficult to agree, complicated to apply and, because of plentiful land-based resources, economically impractical to operate.

Essential Cases

Anglo–Norwegian Fisheries Case (1951): the ICJ upheld Norway's use of straight baselines for its territorial sea because of the "peculiar geography" of the Norwegian coastline, being deeply indented and fringed with islands; the criteria for straight baselines identified by the Court were later, in 1958 and 1982, incorporated into treaties.

North Sea Continental Shelf Cases (1969): the ICJ held that Arts 1–3 of the 1958 Geneva Convention on the Continental Shelf, the core of the continental shelf doctrine, were part of customary law, but that the Convention's formula for delimiting a continental shelf boundary was not; and it then proclaimed the customary formula as requiring equitable delimitation taking account of all relevant circumstances.

Fisheries Jurisdiction Cases (1974): rather timidly, the ICJ declined to pronounce on the extent of a State's exclusive fishing zone because of what it saw as the unsettled nature of international law on the subject; it decided that Iceland could not enforce a zone of 50 miles against the UK and West Germany as their fishermen had traditionally fished in the area.

11 COMMON SPACES

The term "common spaces" is used to refer to those areas subject to international regulation in the interests of the international community. The idea of subjecting particular problem areas to international control is not new. By the Treaty of Versailles of 1919, the strategic port of Danzig (now Gdansk) in the Baltic Sea and its immediate surroundings (population about 350,000) were taken from Germany and placed under the protection of the League of Nations as the Free City of Danzig; much of its internal administration and its foreign affairs were conducted by Poland, but all subject to ultimate control by the League of Nations. The 1947 UN Partition Plan for Palestine proposed a special international regime for Jerusalem, the city to be a *corpus separatum* administered by the UN and distinct from the Jewish and Arab States to be created in Palestine; this plan was not accepted by the parties.

Apart from using international, rather than national, governance for problem areas, some areas call for international co-operation for their optimal utilisation. The Rhine and Danube rivers, for example, pass through a large number of States (seven for the Rhine and 10 for the Danube) and affect the interests of even more. It was recognised in the 19th century that co-operation was necessary for the most effectively use of these rivers. Accordingly, international commissions were established to regulate navigation and other uses of both rivers, these commissions eventually comprising not only the States through which the rivers flow but also non-riparians.

ANTARCTICA

The regulation of common spaces in the common interest gained momentum with the Antarctic Treaty of 1959, governing an area of 5.4 million square miles around the South Pole. The original 12 parties to the treaty intended, in the words of the preamble, to ensure that Antarctica "shall continue forever to be used exclusively for peaceful purposes and shall not become the scene or object of international discord" and to develop co-operation in "the interests of science and the progress of all mankind". To these ends, Antarctica is to be used exclusively for peaceful purposes, with a prohibition on "any measure of a military nature" (Art I) and on any nuclear activity (Art V); freedom of scientific investigation is guaranteed (Art II) and scientific co-operation promoted (Art III), with mutual inspections to ensuring compliance (Art VII). Article IV has the effect of freezing all existing territorial claims to Antarctica (including sector claims as discussed in Chapter 6), providing that there are to be no new claims and that no activities under the treaty were to bolster existing claims.

From this 1959 treaty, which now has 48 parties, has evolved the Antarctic Treaty System (ATS), presaged in Art IX's provision for meetings of the States Parties. This system encompasses more than the bare bones of the Antarctic Treaty, with further agreements on seals in 1972, marine living resources in 1980 and comprehensive environmental protection in 1991. Attempts to permit, but regulate, mineral exploration and exploitation in Antarctica through a treaty in 1988 failed of ratification, and the 1991 environmental protection protocol bans all mining activities.

The ATS is now a general regime regulating the world's fifth largest continent. Its provisions are not now regarded as applying only among the contracting States, but to extend to the entire community of States – an objective international regime in the sense that no State, party or not, can claim territorial rights or undertake military or mining activities in Antarctica.

OUTER SPACE

The launching of the first artificial earth satellite (Sputnik 1) in 1957 in turn launched considerable initiatives in the United Nations to regulate and control activities in outer space. These initiatives resulted in the landmark Outer Space Treaty of 1967, replicating many of the provision of the Antarctic Treaty. Outer space is free for exploration and use, and scientific investigation, by all States (Art 1); the moon and other celestial bodies are not subject to appropriation by any State (Art 2); and there are to be mutual inspections to ensure compliance (Art 12).

States are to notify the UN Secretary-General of any activities in outer space (Art 11), to regard astronauts as "envoys of mankind" and render them all necessary assistance (Art 5), to accept responsibility for all their space activities (Art 6) and to accept liability for damage caused by any of their space objects (Art 7). Some of the provisions of the 1967 Treaty have been fleshed out in subsequent agreements: on the rescue and return of astronauts (1967), the liability for damage caused by space objects (1972), the registration of objects launched into space (1975) and activities on the moon and other celestial bodies (1979).

There are, however, differences between the outer space and the Antarctic regimes. For outer space, while there is a general commitment to its peaceful use, the specific provisions of the 1967 treaty fall short of a blanket prohibition on any and all military activity. The moon and other celestial bodies are to be used for exclusively peaceful purposes, but the same is not the case for outer space, the prohibition being on placing in orbit nuclear weapons and weapons of mass destruction (Art 4). During the Reagan administration (1981–89), the proposed "Star Wars" project was claimed to be a defensive shield against attack and therefore permitted by the 1967 Treaty, a view rejected by the USSR and other States; but the initiative was happily abandoned before this legal claim could be put to any legal test.

While the ATS is a self-contained regime, relying for its rules on what is contained in the various treaties, the regime for outer space, as befits its huge significance for all States, contains more than the contents of the various agreements. All activities in outer space are additionally and explicitly subject to "international law, including the Charter of the United Nations" (Art 3). The ATS is centralised through regular consultative meetings of the (48) States Parties and a dedicated secretariat in Buenos Aires, Argentina. Outer space remains the responsibility of the UN General Assembly, operating though the 69-member UN Committee on the Peaceful Uses of Outer Space (COPUOS), serviced by the UN Office for Outer Space Affairs, part of the UN secretariat.

INTERNATIONAL SEABED AREA

Created by the UN Convention on the Law of the Sea of 1982, this area (discussed in Chapter 10) is the seabed and ocean floor beyond the limits of national jurisdiction (Art 1(1)) in which deep-sea mining is to be regulated. The area and its resources (ie mineral resources *in situ*) are expressed to be "the common heritage of mankind" (Art 136), and activities in the area are to be "carried out for the benefit of mankind as a whole" (Art 140(1)). The area and its resources are not subject to appropriation (Art 137(1)), and the area is open to use exclusively for peaceful purposes (Art 141). Conduct of activities in the area is controlled by the International Seabed Authority, an international organisation, with an Assembly, Council and Secretariat, headquartered at Kingston, Jamaica, and with 160 Member States.

ARCTIC

Until recently, there was little interest in the legal status of the Arctic. Being nothing more than frozen water, with no landmass, the area around the North Pole was, in law, high sea and subject to the regime of the high sea, now codified in the UN Convention on the Law of the Sea. Accordingly, the Arctic outside any of its bordering States' territorial seas was free and open to the vessels of all States and not subject to national appropriation. The prevailing rules about the exclusive economic zone (for fish) and continental shelf (for oil and gas) applied, giving each bordering State a 200-mile fishing zone and a continental shelf extending to at least 200 miles and at most 350 miles (see Chapter 10) – but all that was essentially irrelevant as long as the area within the Arctic Circle remained frozen and unusable for all or most of the year.

Global warming has changed the scenario, raising the prospect of a year-round Northwest Passage for shipping and for the exploitation of Arctic sea-bed hydrocarbons. Canada, with long territorial sea base-lines and consequent large areas claimed as internal waters, will, no doubt, accommodate the needs of international shipping through the Northwest Passage without any need for any new international rules or regime.

Already, a number of States, including Russia and Norway, have made continental shelf claims extending over the Arctic. Given the sensitive environment of the Arctic and the reliance of indigenous peoples on the Arctic's existing resources, one might be tempted to think that some international regime similar to the ATS, outer space or the International Seabed Area would be an ideal solution. That bold and imaginative idea, however, looks likely to be thwarted by the five Arctic circumpolar States, which, in 2008 at Ilulissat, Greenland, formally asserted their "sovereignty, sovereign rights and jurisdiction in large areas of the Arctic Ocean", making them (at least in their own minds) "in a unique position to address these possibilities and challenges". The Ilulissat Declaration recognised the sensitivity of the Arctic ecosystem and the interests of other States and the world community, yet concluded: "We therefore see no need to develop a new comprehensive international legal regime to govern the Arctic Ocean."

Essential Facts

- While not new, the idea of internationalising problem or sensitive areas was given impetus by the 1959 Antarctic Treaty and the Antarctic Treaty System it spawned.
- From the outset, the exploration and use of outer space has been regulated by international law.
- The common heritage of humankind has become a concept applicable to Antarctica and the international seabed area, but will, it appears, not apply in the Arctic.

12 SETTLEMENT OF INTERNATIONAL DISPUTES

The obligation in Art 2(3) of the UN Charter to settle all disputes by peaceful means is fleshed out in Chapter VI of the Charter, Art 33 specifying the options available to States as "negotiation, enquiry, mediation, conciliation, arbitration, judicial settlement, resort to regional agencies or arrangements, or other peaceful means of their own choice". These options do not exactly correspond to the classical methods of dispute settlement in international law.

NEGOTIATIONS

In excess of 90 per cent of all international disputes are settled by direct negotiations between the parties. This is the only method of dispute settlement that does not involve some role for a third party and, as a consequence, is extremely popular with States anxious to retain sovereign control over their own affairs. In addition to their stand-alone role, negotiations can be useful both before and in conjunction with other methods of settling disputes.

GOOD OFFICES

Good offices consist in various kinds of action tending to call negotiations between the disputing States into existence, leaving the settlement to the States and with no role for the person or organ using good offices. The Hague Convention of 1907 for the Pacific Settlement of International Disputes provides that, in any serious disagreement or dispute, the parties agree to submit "to the good offices or mediation" of one or more friendly States; and that good offices and mediation have the exclusive character of advice and never have binding force. The 1907 Hague Convention, and practice in general, tends to blur the distinction between good offices and mediation. While good offices are not mentioned in Art 33(1) of the UN Charter as a means of peaceful settlement of disputes, they has been widely used by the Secretary-General, either on his own initiative or at the behest of the Security Council.

MEDIATION

Mediation involves the participation of a third State or a disinterested individual in negotiations between States in dispute. The role of the mediator is well expressed in Art 4 of the Hague Convention on the Pacific Settlement of Disputes of 1899 as "reconciling the opposing claims and appeasing the feelings of resentment which have arisen between the States at variance".

CONCILIATION

Conciliation has both a broad and a narrow meaning. In its broad sense, it includes the wide range of settlement procedures whereby a dispute is amicably settled with the aid of other States or of impartial commissions of inquiry or advisory committees. In its narrow sense, it means the reference of a dispute to a commission or committee to make a report with proposals to the parties for settlement; these proposals are not binding on the parties.

INQUIRY

An investigation and report by some independent body, often established by or through the UN, on some disputed issue may go a long way to a peaceful settlement of the issue. This was recognised in Art 9 of the 1899 Hague Convention, inquiries being intended "to facilitate a solution of ... differences by elucidating the facts by means of an impartial and conscientious investigation".

In the *Dogger Bank Inquiry* (1905), following the sinking of some British fishing vessels in the North Sea by a Russian fleet panicked by the belief that it was about to be attacked by Japanese submarines, a commission of five naval officers was appointed to ascertain the facts and to pronounce on the responsibility for the incident. The commission reported that there was no justification for the firing upon the fishing vessels and that responsibility lay with the admiral of the Russian fleet. This report of the inquiry reads very much like an arbitral award.

ARBITRATION

Arbitration was used in the Greek city-States and was occasionally resorted to in medieval times, but it was the provisions of the Jay Treaty of 1794 between the US and Great Britain referring to arbitration all the outstanding issues between them that stimulated increased use of arbitration internationally. Further impetus was given by the 1899 and 1907 Hague Conventions for the Pacific Settlement of International Disputes, the former also establishing the Permanent Court of Arbitration. The PCA is not an actual tribunal, but consists in an International Bureau at The Hague serving as registry, and a panel made up by the appointment by each contracting State of four suitably qualified persons, from which States wishing to have recourse to the Court may each choose two arbiters, who in turn select an umpire. Despite having over 100 parties to one or both of the Hague Conventions, the PCA has not been extensively utilised, though arbitration as a means of settling international disputes has remained popular.

Submission to arbitration is a voluntary act on the part of a State. This submission will invariably be contained in a treaty, concluded either generally or in respect of a particular dispute; and it will be contained in a compromissary clause, or *compromis*. A *compromis* would typically specify the issues in dispute, the composition of the arbitral tribunal, the law to be applied, the procedure to be followed and the effect of the eventual decision (called an award). Much, then, is in the hands of States. By formulating the issues, the parties can focus on what they see as the precise differences between them. By selecting the arbiters, they can ensure that they have their nationals on the tribunal. They might, exceptionally, have faith in a single arbiter, as in the *Island of Palmas Arbitration* (1928), in which the US and the Netherlands appointed the renowned Max Huber, or, more usually, they will each appoint an arbiter (or perhaps two) along with a further arbiter or arbiters to guarantee that the tribunal cannot be equally divided. For the *Anglo–French Continental Shelf Case* (1978), the parties each appointed its own national judge on the ICJ along with three other ICJ judges of other nationalities.

The parties also determine the law to be applied by the tribunal. In the absence of a specific choice of law, international law is to be applied. The authoritative value in international law of any arbitration depends on that choice of law, an award having no value if the law being applied is not international law. In the *Texaco–Libya Arbitration* (1977), the terms of the concession contract that was the basis of the arbitration required the sole arbiter to apply "the principles of the law of Libya common to the principles of international law and in the absence of such common principles then by and in accordance with the general principles of law, including such of these principles as may have been by international tribunals". What value would an award using that incomprehensible formula have in international law? Fortunately, the arbiter, René-Jean Dupuy, interpreted the formula to mean international custom, thus making his award an important authority on the law relating to expropriation.

The parties likewise determine the procedure to be followed, usually allowing one or two written submissions by each party, followed by oral submissions. The effect of the award will be agreed between the parties, usually declaring the award to be final and without any further appeal.

The great attraction of arbitration, particularly as against judicial settlement, lies in the latitude afforded to the States to keep substantial control over the proceedings. An award is made by their tribunal deciding their issues in accordance with their law and procedure. Further, arbitration will generally be cheaper and quicker than any judicial settlement.

JUDICIAL SETTLEMENT

There are today a number of international courts but only one, the International Court of Justice, can be regarded as a world court. The other international courts are either subject-specific, such as the International Criminal Court (see Chapter 9) and the International Tribunal for the Law of the Sea; or regional and subject-specific, such as the European Court of Justice (of the European Union), the European Court of Human Rights (see Chapter 9) and the Inter-American Court of Human Rights. The ICJ alone has general competence ranging over all of international law, that competence, as expressed in Art 36(2) of its Statute, extending to:

(a) the interpretation of a treaty;

(b) any question of international law;

(c) the existence of any fact which, if established, would constitute a breach of an international obligation;

(d) the nature or extent of the reparation to be made for the breach of an international obligation.

Permanent Court of International Justice

Following calls for the creation of a permanent international court, spurred by the successes of international arbitration in the 19th and early 20th centuries, the Permanent Court of International Justice was established pursuant to Art 14 of the Covenant of the League of Nations. The Council of the League appointed a Committee of Jurists to draft a Statute and that Statute was approved by the Assembly in December 1920. The Court formally opened in February 1922, and closed, with the resignation of the judges, on 31 January 1946.

The PCIJ is the direct predecessor of the International Court of Justice. Decisions of the PCIJ are collected in *PCIJ, Ser A* (Judgments 1922–30), *PCIJ, Ser B* (Advisory Opinions 1922–30), and *PCIJ, Ser A/B* (Judgments, Orders and Advisory Opinions 1930–40); the major decisions are gathered in Hudson, *World Court Reports* (4 vols, 1934–38); and are available online with the reports of the ICJ at www.icj-cij.org.

International Court of Justice

With the demise of the League of Nations and the creation of the United Nations, it was decided to set up a new permanent international court. The International Court of Justice was established as *a* principal organ of the UN by Art 7 of the UN Charter and, under Art 92, it is *the* principal judicial organ of the organisation. That latter article provides further that the Court is to function in accordance with its Statute, annexed to the Charter, and stated expressly both to be based on the Statute of the Permanent Court of International Justice and to form an integral part of the Charter. All members of the UN are *ipso facto* parties to the ICJ Statute (Art 93). Like its predecessor, the ICJ is located at the Peace Palace in The Hague.

The Court's decisions and opinions are published in the *International Court of Justice Reports (ICJ Rep)*. The Court also publishes the *Pleadings, Oral Arguments and Documents* in any proceedings before it; its Rules of Court appear in a series entitled *Acts and Documents concerning the Organisation of the Court*, as well as successive numbers of the *International Court of Justice Yearbook*, containing, incidentally, an exhaustive bibliography of the Court. Links to, and information about, the Court and all its contentious decisions and advisory opinions are available online at www.icj-cij.org.

Composition of the Court

"The Court shall be composed of a body of independent judges, elected regardless of their nationality from among persons of high moral character, who possess the qualifications required in their respective countries for appointment to the highest judicial offices, or are jurisconsults of recognized competence in international law": ICJ Statute, Art 2. The ICJ has 15 judges (Art 3(1)), elected for a term of 9 years, and eligible for re-election (Art 13(1)). The terms of judges are staggered to ensure continuity on the Bench, five judges completing their terms every 3 years.

No two judges can be nationals of the same State (Art 3). To ensure suitably qualified judges, candidates for the Court are nominated, after consultations with the highest court of justice, law faculties and schools of law, and national academies and national sections of international academies devoted to the study of law in each State, by national groups in the Permanent Court of Arbitration or *ad hoc* national groups (Arts 4–6). The General Assembly and Security Council, acting independently of one another, elect candidates to membership of the Court by an absolute majority of votes in each organ (Art 10.)

The five permanent members of the Security Council have always had a judge of their nationality on the Court. The present composition of the Court has a judge from each of the permanent members (from the UK, Christopher Greenwood); the 10 other judges come from Brazil, Germany, Japan, Jordan, Mexico, Morocco, New Zealand, Sierra Leone, Slovakia and Somalia.

The independence of the members of the Court is secured in a member of ways. ICJ judges are prohibited from exercising any political or administrative function, from engaging in any other profession (Arts 15–16) and from acting as agent, counsel or advocate in any case (Art 17). Before taking office, each judge must solemnly undertake to act "impartially and conscientiously" (Art 20).

One of the distinctive features of the ICJ is that any party to a dispute which does not have a national as a member of the Court may appoint an *ad hoc* judge (Art 31). *Ad hoc* judges are frequently appointed: in its annual report for 2009, the Court records that 25 parties had appointed *ad hoc* judges in that year. While the institution of judges *ad hoc* has been criticised as detracting from the true international character of the Court and as potentially disruptive of the collegiality of the bench, it is better justified as increasing the judicial resources available to the Court and as necessary in contemporary world politics.

The ICJ generally sits as Full Bench, where the quorum is nine judges, excluding *ad hoc* judges, (Art 25), but it now has the power under Arts 26–29 of its Statute to sit in chambers of at least three judges, the decisions of these chambers being equivalent to those of the plenary Court. Two types of chambers are contemplated by Art 26: chambers for special categories of cases, "such as labour or communications"; and *ad hoc* chambers to hear particular disputes. In 1993, a Chamber for Environmental Matters was established, only to be mothballed 13 years later because no cases had been referred to it. *Ad hoc* chambers are more frequently convened. In the *Gulf of Maine Case* (1984), an *ad hoc* chamber was constituted to determine a maritime boundary dispute between the US and Canada; the parties insisted on the appointment of judges to the chamber acceptable to them.

In introducing chambers into ICJ practice in 1978, the hope was that more cases would be referred to the Court. However, there has been criticism that the use of chambers has reduced the ICJ to something close to an arbitral proceeding and that a chamber (of three or five judges) cannot authoritatively pronounce on rules of universal international law from the legal-cultural perspectives available in the full 15-member Court.

Contentious jurisdiction

The ICJ has two limbs of jurisdiction: in contentious cases between States; and in advisory opinions at the instance of the United Nations and other international organisations. Any dispute about the Court's jurisdiction falls to be determined by the Court itself (Art 36(6)), reflecting a rule common to all UN organs that they determine their own jurisdiction or competence.

Only States may be parties to contentious cases before the Court (Art 34(1)); the Court is open to those States which are parties to the Statute (Art 35(1)) and, on conditions laid down by the Security Council, to other States also (Art 35(2)–(3)). Chapter II of the Statute, which bears the title "Competence of the Court", deals with its jurisdiction in contentious cases, making it abundantly clear that the Court has jurisdiction only with the consent of the States parties to a dispute. As was said in the *Interpretation of the Peace Treaties Opinion* (1950), "The consent of States, parties to a dispute, is the basis of the Court's jurisdiction in contentious cases".

Contentious jurisdiction is governed by two paragraphs of Art 36 of the Statute. Under Art 36(1),

> The jurisdiction of the Court comprises all cases which the parties refer to it and all matters specially provided for in the Charter of the United Nations or in treaties and conventions in force.

Thus, first, States may agree *ad hoc* to the submission of a dispute to the Court. In the *Minquiers and Ecrohos Case* (1953), the UK and France, in a special agreement of 1950, submitted to the ICJ their dispute on the sovereignty over two island groups in the Bay of Biscay; in the *Gabčikovo Nagymaros Project Case* (1997), Hungary and Slovakia, in a special agreement of 1993, submitted to the ICJ their dispute about a hydro-electric project on the Danube.

Secondly, while Art 36(1) talks of the Court having jurisdiction in matters specially provided for in the Charter, there is no such special provision. The Statute of the ICJ was adopted before the UN Charter was concluded, and the anticipated special provision in the Charter did not make it to the document signed at San Francisco in June 1945.

Thirdly, jurisdiction may arise from a commitment in treaties that all future disputes as to their interpretation and application be referred to the Court. There are over 300 bilateral and multilateral treaties conferring jurisdiction on the Court. The ICJ had jurisdiction in the US/Iran *Tehran Hostages Case* (1980), through the Optional Protocols to the Vienna Conventions of Diplomatic and on Consular Relations of 1961 and 1963 and through a bilateral Treaty of Amity, Economic Relations, and Consular Rights of 1955. In the *Fisheries Jurisdiction Cases* (1974), the ICJ had jurisdiction through the undertaking in an Exchange of Notes of 1961 between Iceland and the UK that any further extension of Iceland's fishery limits could be referred to the Court at the instance of the UK.

Article 36(2), the so-called "Optional Clause", was intended to give the ICJ something closer to compulsory jurisdiction. It reads:

> "The States Parties to the present Statute may at any time declare that they recognize as compulsory *ipso facto* and without special agreement, in relation to any other State accepting the same obligation, the jurisdiction of the Court in all legal disputes ..."

Article 36(2) jurisdiction is based on a unilateral declaration by a State that it accepts the jurisdiction of the Court. Such a declaration will invariably expressly provide, as Art 36(3) anticipates, that it is based on reciprocity – on another State accepting the same obligation. Indeed, reciprocity is at the very core of Art 36(2) jurisdiction. "Jurisdiction is conferred on the Court only to the extent to which the two declarations coincide in conferring it": *Phosphates in Morocco Case* (1938). Given that declarations are usually replete with reservations as to subject-matter excluded from the Court's jurisdiction, the initial task of the Court is to determine whether the two declarations in fact coincide. The result is that, while a State can exclude jurisdiction through a reservation in its own declaration, because of reciprocity, it can invoke a reservation in the other party's declaration to exclude jurisdiction. In the *Norwegian Loans Case* (1957), Norway, the respondent State, successfully challenged the jurisdiction of the Court on the basis of a reservation in the French declaration.

One particular common reservation is of doubtful validity. Some States have purported to exclude the Court's jurisdiction in matters of domestic jurisdiction as understood by the reserving State, opening the door to the possibility of that State objecting to virtually any jurisdiction under Art 36(2). While the Court has not ruled on the validity of subjective domestic jurisdiction reservations, they run counter to the power of the Court under Art 36(6) to determine its own jurisdiction. *Dicta* by some judges in the *Norwegian Loans Case* questioned the validity of this type of reservation, suggesting that it either invalidated the entire declaration or, invalid in itself, might be severed from the rest of the declaration.

In all, only 66 States have made Art 36(2) declarations; the UK is the only permanent member of the Security Council to have an extant declaration. The US withdrew its 1946 declaration in October 1985 in consequence of the decision in the jurisdictional phase of the *Military and Paramilitary Activities Case* (1986).

The judgment of the ICJ in a contentious case is "final and without appeal" (Art 60). Under Art 94 of the UN Charter, each State must comply with the decision of the Court in any case in which it is party; and, in the event of non-compliance, the Security Council may make recommendations or decide upon measures to give effect to a judgment.

Article 59 of the ICJ Statute, providing that a decision has "no binding force except between the parties and in respect of that particular case", achieves two goals: it applies the common municipal principle of *res judicata* (a matter once decided cannot be re-litigated by the same parties); and it excludes from the jurisprudence of the ICJ the Anglo–American concept of judicial precedent. That said, there are limited circumstance (the emergence of crucial new facts) in which the Court may review a decision (Art 61); and the Court, in practice, frequently cites and founds upon earlier decisions in determining later cases.

Advisory jurisdiction

"The Court of Justice may give an advisory opinion on any legal question at the request of whatever body may be authorized by or in accordance with the Charter of the United Nations to make such a request": Art 65(1) of the ICJ Statute. The General Assembly and the Security Council are authorised to request advisory opinions (Art 96(1) of the UN Charter). Under Art 96(2), ECOSOC, the (now moribund) Trusteeship Council, the Interim Committee of the General Assembly, and all but one of the UN's Specialised Agencies (16 in number, the exception being the Universal Postal Union), have been authorised by the General Assembly to request advisory opinions. Advisory opinions are of their nature not binding in law, though they may establish principles of law that are followed in subsequent cases and opinions.

The ICJ is not obliged to give an advisory opinion; the wording of Art 65(1) of the Statute leaves the Court a discretion. The Court has indicated that it will decline a request for an advisory opinion only if there are "compelling reasons" to do so: *Western Sahara Case* (1975). The Court will not give an advisory opinion where the request concerns a matter which is in reality a contentious dispute between States or concerns essentially factual matters and a State concerned refuses to co-operate, thereby making it "very doubtful whether there would be available to the

Court materials sufficient to enable it to arrive at any judicial conclusion upon the question of fact": *Eastern Carelia Opinion* (1923). Nor will the Court give an advisory opinion where the request by a Specialised Agency falls outside the scope of its activities, as happened with the World Health Organization's request for an advisory opinion on the legality of nuclear weapons: *Legality of the Use by a State of Nuclear Weapons in Armed Conflict* (1996).

Essential Facts

- As the judicial settlement of international disputes plays a more limited role than courts in municipal law, informal settlement procedures have been developed in international law.
- The scope and effect of any international arbitration are wholly dependent on the terms of the disputing States' agreement to submit to arbitration.
- The International Court of Justice has jurisdiction in contentious cases, open only to States on the basis of their voluntary submission to jurisdiction.
- The ICJ may give advisory opinions, but only at the request of an authorised organ of the UN or Specialised Agency.

Essential Cases

Norwegian Loans Case (1957): while emphasising that submission to its jurisdiction was a voluntary act, the ICJ held that it did not have jurisdiction because Norway could rely on a reservation in the French submission to jurisdiction excluding matters which were essentially within the domestic jurisdiction of France as understood by France.

Eastern Carelia Opinion (1923): the PCIJ declined to give an advisory opinion because the request related to an actual dispute between States; and, through the non-appearance of one of the States closely involved, information essential to the determination of the opinion would not be available to the Court.

INDEX